When I retire at night...

Chronology of today's events:

___

Was I resentful?
- 1. Who/what
- 2. Cause
- 3. Affects
- 4. My part

Was I selfish?

Was I dishonest?

Was I afraid?

Do I owe an apology?

What have I wrongly kept secret?

Was I kind and loving toward all?

What could I have done better?

How did faith or fear rule my actions today?

Today I gave of my time ___, talent ___, treasure ___, and touch ___.

Who did I help today?

What am I grateful for today?

Who needs my prayers today?

God, forgive me where I have been resentful, selfish, dishonest, or afraid today. Help me not to keep anything to myself, but to discuss it openly with another person. Show me where I owe an apology and help me make it, and help me to be kind and loving to all people. Use me in the mainstream of life, and remove worry, remorse, and morbid reflection that I may be of service to others. Amen.

When I retire at night...   /   /

Chronology of today's events:

Was I resentful?
    1. Who/what   3. Affects

    2. Cause   4. My part

Was I selfish?

Was I dishonest?

Was I afraid?

Do I owe an apology?

What have I wrongly kept secret?

Was I kind and loving toward all?

What could I have done better?

How did faith or fear rule my actions today?

Today I gave of my time ___, talent ___, treasure ___, and touch ___.

Who did I help today?

What am I grateful for today?

Who needs my prayers today?

God, forgive me where I have been resentful, selfish, dishonest, or afraid today. Help me not to keep anything to myself, but to discuss it openly with another person. Show me where I owe an apology and help me make it, and help me to be kind and loving to all people. Use me in the mainstream of life, and remove worry, remorse, and morbid reflection that I may be of service to others. Amen.

When I retire at night...   /   /

Chronology of today's events:

Was I resentful?
    1. *Who/what*   3. *Affects*

    2. *Cause*   4. *My part*

Was I selfish?

Was I dishonest?

Was I afraid?

Do I owe an apology?

What have I wrongly kept secret?

Was I kind and loving toward all?

What could I have done better?

How did faith or fear rule my actions today?

Today I gave of my time ___, talent ___, treasure ___, and touch ___.

Who did I help today?

What am I grateful for today?

Who needs my prayers today?

God, forgive me where I have been resentful, selfish, dishonest, or afraid today. Help me not to keep anything to myself, but to discuss it openly with another person. Show me where I owe an apology and help me make it, and help me to be kind and loving to all people. Use me in the mainstream of life, and remove worry, remorse, and morbid reflection that I may be of service to others. Amen.

When I retire at night...   /   /

Chronology of today's events:

Was I resentful?
    1. *Who/what*   3. *Affects*

    2. *Cause*   4. *My part*

Was I selfish?

Was I dishonest?

Was I afraid?

Do I owe an apology?

What have I wrongly kept secret?

Was I kind and loving toward all?

What could I have done better?

How did faith or fear rule my actions today?

Today I gave of my time ___, talent ___, treasure ___, and touch ___.

Who did I help today?

What am I grateful for today?

Who needs my prayers today?

God, forgive me where I have been resentful, selfish, dishonest, or afraid today. Help me not to keep anything to myself, but to discuss it openly with another person. Show me where I owe an apology and help me make it, and help me to be kind and loving to all people. Use me in the mainstream of life, and remove worry, remorse, and morbid reflection that I may be of service to others. Amen.

When I retire at night...   /   /

Chronology of today's events:

Was I resentful?
    1. *Who/what*   3. *Affects*

    2. *Cause*   4. *My part*

Was I selfish?

Was I dishonest?

Was I afraid?

Do I owe an apology?

What have I wrongly kept secret?

Was I kind and loving toward all?

What could I have done better?

How did faith or fear rule my actions today?

Today I gave of my time ___, talent ___, treasure ___, and touch ___.

Who did I help today?

What am I grateful for today?

Who needs my prayers today?

God, forgive me where I have been resentful, selfish, dishonest, or afraid today. Help me not to keep anything to myself, but to discuss it openly with another person. Show me where I owe an apology and help me make it, and help me to be kind and loving to all people. Use me in the mainstream of life, and remove worry, remorse, and morbid reflection that I may be of service to others. Amen.

When I retire at night…   /   /

Chronology of today's events:

Was I resentful?
    1. *Who/what*   3.   *Affects*

    2. *Cause*   4.   *My part*

Was I selfish?

Was I dishonest?

Was I afraid?

Do I owe an apology?

What have I wrongly kept secret?

Was I kind and loving toward all?

What could I have done better?

How did faith or fear rule my actions today?

Today I gave of my time ___, talent ___, treasure ___, and touch ___.

Who did I help today?

What am I grateful for today?

Who needs my prayers today?

God, forgive me where I have been resentful, selfish, dishonest, or afraid today. Help me not to keep anything to myself, but to discuss it openly with another person. Show me where I owe an apology and help me make it, and help me to be kind and loving to all people. Use me in the mainstream of life, and remove worry, remorse, and morbid reflection that I may be of service to others. Amen.

When I retire at night...   /   /

Chronology of today's events:

_____
_____

Was I resentful?
    1. *Who/what*   3. *Affects*

    2. *Cause*   4. *My part*

Was I selfish?

Was I dishonest?

Was I afraid?

Do I owe an apology?

What have I wrongly kept secret?

Was I kind and loving toward all?

What could I have done better?

How did faith or fear rule my actions today?

Today I gave of my time ___, talent ___, treasure ___, and touch ___.

Who did I help today?

What am I grateful for today?

Who needs my prayers today?

God, forgive me where I have been resentful, selfish, dishonest, or afraid today. Help me not to keep anything to myself, but to discuss it openly with another person. Show me where I owe an apology and help me make it, and help me to be kind and loving to all people. Use me in the mainstream of life, and remove worry, remorse, and morbid reflection that I may be of service to others. Amen.

When I retire at night...   /   /

Chronology of today's events:

Was I resentful?
    1. Who/what   3. Affects

    2. Cause   4. My part

Was I selfish?

Was I dishonest?

Was I afraid?

Do I owe an apology?

What have I wrongly kept secret?

Was I kind and loving toward all?

What could I have done better?

How did faith or fear rule my actions today?

Today I gave of my time ___, talent ___, treasure ___, and touch ___.

Who did I help today?

What am I grateful for today?

Who needs my prayers today?

God, forgive me where I have been resentful, selfish, dishonest, or afraid today. Help me not to keep anything to myself, but to discuss it openly with another person. Show me where I owe an apology and help me make it, and help me to be kind and loving to all people. Use me in the mainstream of life, and remove worry, remorse, and morbid reflection that I may be of service to others. Amen.

When I retire at night...   /   /

Chronology of today's events:

Was I resentful?

    1. *Who/what*   3. *Affects*

    2. *Cause*   4. *My part*

Was I selfish?

Was I dishonest?

Was I afraid?

Do I owe an apology?

What have I wrongly kept secret?

Was I kind and loving toward all?

What could I have done better?

How did faith or fear rule my actions today?

Today I gave of my time ___, talent ___, treasure ___, and touch ___.

Who did I help today?

What am I grateful for today?

Who needs my prayers today?

God, forgive me where I have been resentful, selfish, dishonest, or afraid today. Help me not to keep anything to myself, but to discuss it openly with another person. Show me where I owe an apology and help me make it, and help me to be kind and loving to all people. Use me in the mainstream of life, and remove worry, remorse, and morbid reflection that I may be of service to others. Amen.

When I retire at night...   /   /

Chronology of today's events:

Was I resentful?
   1. *Who/what*   3. *Affects*
   2. *Cause*   4. *My part*

Was I selfish?

Was I dishonest?

Was I afraid?

Do I owe an apology?

What have I wrongly kept secret?

Was I kind and loving toward all?

What could I have done better?

How did faith or fear rule my actions today?

Today I gave of my time ___, talent ___, treasure ___, and touch ___.

Who did I help today?

What am I grateful for today?

Who needs my prayers today?

God, forgive me where I have been resentful, selfish, dishonest, or afraid today. Help me not to keep anything to myself, but to discuss it openly with another person. Show me where I owe an apology and help me make it, and help me to be kind and loving to all people. Use me in the mainstream of life, and remove worry, remorse, and morbid reflection that I may be of service to others. Amen.

When I retire at night...   /   /

Chronology of today's events:

_____
_____

Was I resentful?
    1. *Who/what*   3.   *Affects*

    2. *Cause*   4.   *My part*

Was I selfish?

Was I dishonest?

Was I afraid?

Do I owe an apology?

What have I wrongly kept secret?

Was I kind and loving toward all?

What could I have done better?

How did faith or fear rule my actions today?

Today I gave of my time ___, talent ___, treasure ___, and touch ___.

Who did I help today?

What am I grateful for today?

Who needs my prayers today?

God, forgive me where I have been resentful, selfish, dishonest, or afraid today. Help me not to keep anything to myself, but to discuss it openly with another person. Show me where I owe an apology and help me make it, and help me to be kind and loving to all people. Use me in the mainstream of life, and remove worry, remorse, and morbid reflection that I may be of service to others. Amen.

When I retire at night…   /   /

Chronology of today's events:

Was I resentful?
    1. *Who/what*   3. *Affects*

    2. *Cause*   4. *My part*

Was I selfish?

Was I dishonest?

Was I afraid?

Do I owe an apology?

What have I wrongly kept secret?

Was I kind and loving toward all?

What could I have done better?

How did faith or fear rule my actions today?

Today I gave of my time ___, talent ___, treasure ___, and touch ___.

Who did I help today?

What am I grateful for today?

Who needs my prayers today?

God, forgive me where I have been resentful, selfish, dishonest, or afraid today. Help me not to keep anything to myself, but to discuss it openly with another person. Show me where I owe an apology and help me make it, and help me to be kind and loving to all people. Use me in the mainstream of life, and remove worry, remorse, and morbid reflection that I may be of service to others. Amen.

When I retire at night...   /   /

Chronology of today's events:

Was I resentful?
    1. *Who/what*   3. *Affects*

    2. *Cause*   4. *My part*

Was I selfish?

Was I dishonest?

Was I afraid?

Do I owe an apology?

What have I wrongly kept secret?

Was I kind and loving toward all?

What could I have done better?

How did faith or fear rule my actions today?

Today I gave of my time ___, talent ___, treasure ___, and touch ___.

Who did I help today?

What am I grateful for today?

Who needs my prayers today?

God, forgive me where I have been resentful, selfish, dishonest, or afraid today. Help me not to keep anything to myself, but to discuss it openly with another person. Show me where I owe an apology and help me make it, and help me to be kind and loving to all people. Use me in the mainstream of life, and remove worry, remorse, and morbid reflection that I may be of service to others. Amen.

When I retire at night...   /   /

Chronology of today's events:

Was I resentful?
    1. Who/what   3. Affects

    2. Cause   4. My part

Was I selfish?

Was I dishonest?

Was I afraid?

Do I owe an apology?

What have I wrongly kept secret?

Was I kind and loving toward all?

What could I have done better?

How did faith or fear rule my actions today?

Today I gave of my time ___, talent ___, treasure ___, and touch ___.

Who did I help today?

What am I grateful for today?

Who needs my prayers today?

God, forgive me where I have been resentful, selfish, dishonest, or afraid today. Help me not to keep anything to myself, but to discuss it openly with another person. Show me where I owe an apology and help me make it, and help me to be kind and loving to all people. Use me in the mainstream of life, and remove worry, remorse, and morbid reflection that I may be of service to others. Amen.

When I retire at night...   /   /

Chronology of today's events:

Was I resentful?
  1. *Who/what*   3. *Affects*
  2. *Cause*   4. *My part*

Was I selfish?

Was I dishonest?

Was I afraid?

Do I owe an apology?

What have I wrongly kept secret?

Was I kind and loving toward all?

What could I have done better?

How did faith or fear rule my actions today?

Today I gave of my time ___, talent ___, treasure ___, and touch ___.

Who did I help today?

What am I grateful for today?

Who needs my prayers today?

God, forgive me where I have been resentful, selfish, dishonest, or afraid today. Help me not to keep anything to myself, but to discuss it openly with another person. Show me where I owe an apology and help me make it, and help me to be kind and loving to all people. Use me in the mainstream of life, and remove worry, remorse, and morbid reflection that I may be of service to others. Amen.

When I retire at night...   /   /

Chronology of today's events:

Was I resentful?
    1. *Who/what*   3. *Affects*

    2. *Cause*   4. *My part*

Was I selfish?

Was I dishonest?

Was I afraid?

Do I owe an apology?

What have I wrongly kept secret?

Was I kind and loving toward all?

What could I have done better?

How did faith or fear rule my actions today?

Today I gave of my time ___, talent ___, treasure ___, and touch ___.

Who did I help today?

What am I grateful for today?

Who needs my prayers today?

God, forgive me where I have been resentful, selfish, dishonest, or afraid today. Help me not to keep anything to myself, but to discuss it openly with another person. Show me where I owe an apology and help me make it, and help me to be kind and loving to all people. Use me in the mainstream of life, and remove worry, remorse, and morbid reflection that I may be of service to others. Amen.

When I retire at night...   /   /

Chronology of today's events:

Was I resentful?
    1. *Who/what*   3.   *Affects*

    2. *Cause*   4.   *My part*

Was I selfish?

Was I dishonest?

Was I afraid?

Do I owe an apology?

What have I wrongly kept secret?

Was I kind and loving toward all?

What could I have done better?

How did faith or fear rule my actions today?

Today I gave of my time ___, talent ___, treasure ___, and touch ___.

Who did I help today?

What am I grateful for today?

Who needs my prayers today?

God, forgive me where I have been resentful, selfish, dishonest, or afraid today. Help me not to keep anything to myself, but to discuss it openly with another person. Show me where I owe an apology and help me make it, and help me to be kind and loving to all people. Use me in the mainstream of life, and remove worry, remorse, and morbid reflection that I may be of service to others. Amen.

When I retire at night...   /   /

Chronology of today's events:

Was I resentful?
    1. *Who/what*   3. *Affects*

    2. *Cause*   4. *My part*

Was I selfish?

Was I dishonest?

Was I afraid?

Do I owe an apology?

What have I wrongly kept secret?

Was I kind and loving toward all?

What could I have done better?

How did faith or fear rule my actions today?

Today I gave of my time ___, talent ___, treasure ___, and touch ___.

Who did I help today?

What am I grateful for today?

Who needs my prayers today?

God, forgive me where I have been resentful, selfish, dishonest, or afraid today. Help me not to keep anything to myself, but to discuss it openly with another person. Show me where I owe an apology and help me make it, and help me to be kind and loving to all people. Use me in the mainstream of life, and remove worry, remorse, and morbid reflection that I may be of service to others. Amen.

When I retire at night...   /   /

Chronology of today's events:

Was I resentful?
    1. *Who/what*   3. *Affects*

    2. *Cause*   4. *My part*

Was I selfish?

Was I dishonest?

Was I afraid?

Do I owe an apology?

What have I wrongly kept secret?

Was I kind and loving toward all?

What could I have done better?

How did faith or fear rule my actions today?

Today I gave of my time ___, talent ___, treasure ___, and touch ___.

Who did I help today?

What am I grateful for today?

Who needs my prayers today?

God, forgive me where I have been resentful, selfish, dishonest, or afraid today. Help me not to keep anything to myself, but to discuss it openly with another person. Show me where I owe an apology and help me make it, and help me to be kind and loving to all people. Use me in the mainstream of life, and remove worry, remorse, and morbid reflection that I may be of service to others. Amen.

When I retire at night…   /   /

Chronology of today's events:

Was I resentful?
- 1. *Who/what*
- 2. *Cause*
- 3. *Affects*
- 4. *My part*

Was I selfish?

Was I dishonest?

Was I afraid?

Do I owe an apology?

What have I wrongly kept secret?

Was I kind and loving toward all?

What could I have done better?

How did faith or fear rule my actions today?

Today I gave of my time ___, talent ___, treasure ___, and touch ___.

Who did I help today?

What am I grateful for today?

Who needs my prayers today?

God, forgive me where I have been resentful, selfish, dishonest, or afraid today. Help me not to keep anything to myself, but to discuss it openly with another person. Show me where I owe an apology and help me make it, and help me to be kind and loving to all people. Use me in the mainstream of life, and remove worry, remorse, and morbid reflection that I may be of service to others. Amen.

When I retire at night...   /   /

Chronology of today's events:

Was I resentful?
    1. *Who/what*   3. *Affects*

    2. *Cause*   4. *My part*

Was I selfish?

Was I dishonest?

Was I afraid?

Do I owe an apology?

What have I wrongly kept secret?

Was I kind and loving toward all?

What could I have done better?

How did faith or fear rule my actions today?

Today I gave of my time ___, talent ___, treasure ___, and touch ___.

Who did I help today?

What am I grateful for today?

Who needs my prayers today?

God, forgive me where I have been resentful, selfish, dishonest, or afraid today. Help me not to keep anything to myself, but to discuss it openly with another person. Show me where I owe an apology and help me make it, and help me to be kind and loving to all people. Use me in the mainstream of life, and remove worry, remorse, and morbid reflection that I may be of service to others. Amen.

When I retire at night...   /   /

Chronology of today's events:

Was I resentful?
    1. *Who/what*   3. *Affects*

    2. *Cause*   4. *My part*

Was I selfish?

Was I dishonest?

Was I afraid?

Do I owe an apology?

What have I wrongly kept secret?

Was I kind and loving toward all?

What could I have done better?

How did faith or fear rule my actions today?

Today I gave of my time ___, talent ___, treasure ___, and touch ___.

Who did I help today?

What am I grateful for today?

Who needs my prayers today?

God, forgive me where I have been resentful, selfish, dishonest, or afraid today. Help me not to keep anything to myself, but to discuss it openly with another person. Show me where I owe an apology and help me make it, and help me to be kind and loving to all people. Use me in the mainstream of life, and remove worry, remorse, and morbid reflection that I may be of service to others. Amen.

When I retire at night...   /   /

Chronology of today's events:

Was I resentful?
    1. Who/what   *3. Affects*

    2. Cause   *4. My part*

Was I selfish?

Was I dishonest?

Was I afraid?

Do I owe an apology?

What have I wrongly kept secret?

Was I kind and loving toward all?

What could I have done better?

How did faith or fear rule my actions today?

Today I gave of my time ___, talent ___, treasure ___, and touch ___.

Who did I help today?

What am I grateful for today?

Who needs my prayers today?

God, forgive me where I have been resentful, selfish, dishonest, or afraid today. Help me not to keep anything to myself, but to discuss it openly with another person. Show me where I owe an apology and help me make it, and help me to be kind and loving to all people. Use me in the mainstream of life, and remove worry, remorse, and morbid reflection that I may be of service to others. Amen.

When I retire at night...   /   /

Chronology of today's events:

Was I resentful?
    1. *Who/what*   3. *Affects*

    2. *Cause*   4. *My part*

Was I selfish?

Was I dishonest?

Was I afraid?

Do I owe an apology?

What have I wrongly kept secret?

Was I kind and loving toward all?

What could I have done better?

How did faith or fear rule my actions today?

Today I gave of my time ____, talent ____, treasure ____, and touch ____.

Who did I help today?

What am I grateful for today?

Who needs my prayers today?

God, forgive me where I have been resentful, selfish, dishonest, or afraid today. Help me not to keep anything to myself, but to discuss it openly with another person. Show me where I owe an apology and help me make it, and help me to be kind and loving to all people. Use me in the mainstream of life, and remove worry, remorse, and morbid reflection that I may be of service to others. Amen.

When I retire at night...   /   /

Chronology of today's events:

Was I resentful?
    1. *Who/what*   3. *Affects*

    2. *Cause*   4. *My part*

Was I selfish?

Was I dishonest?

Was I afraid?

Do I owe an apology?

What have I wrongly kept secret?

Was I kind and loving toward all?

What could I have done better?

How did faith or fear rule my actions today?

Today I gave of my time ___, talent ___, treasure ___, and touch ___.

Who did I help today?

What am I grateful for today?

Who needs my prayers today?

God, forgive me where I have been resentful, selfish, dishonest, or afraid today. Help me not to keep anything to myself, but to discuss it openly with another person. Show me where I owe an apology and help me make it, and help me to be kind and loving to all people. Use me in the mainstream of life, and remove worry, remorse, and morbid reflection that I may be of service to others. Amen.

When I retire at night...   /   /

Chronology of today's events:

Was I resentful?
    1. Who/what   *3. Affects*

    2. Cause   *4. My part*

Was I selfish?

Was I dishonest?

Was I afraid?

Do I owe an apology?

What have I wrongly kept secret?

Was I kind and loving toward all?

What could I have done better?

How did faith or fear rule my actions today?

Today I gave of my time ___, talent ___, treasure ___, and touch ___.

Who did I help today?

What am I grateful for today?

Who needs my prayers today?

God, forgive me where I have been resentful, selfish, dishonest, or afraid today. Help me not to keep anything to myself, but to discuss it openly with another person. Show me where I owe an apology and help me make it, and help me to be kind and loving to all people. Use me in the mainstream of life, and remove worry, remorse, and morbid reflection that I may be of service to others. Amen.

When I retire at night...   /   /

Chronology of today's events:

Was I resentful?
    1. *Who/what*   3. *Affects*

    2. *Cause*   4. *My part*

Was I selfish?

Was I dishonest?

Was I afraid?

Do I owe an apology?

What have I wrongly kept secret?

Was I kind and loving toward all?

What could I have done better?

How did faith or fear rule my actions today?

Today I gave of my time ___, talent ___, treasure ___, and touch ___.

Who did I help today?

What am I grateful for today?

Who needs my prayers today?

God, forgive me where I have been resentful, selfish, dishonest, or afraid today. Help me not to keep anything to myself, but to discuss it openly with another person. Show me where I owe an apology and help me make it, and help me to be kind and loving to all people. Use me in the mainstream of life, and remove worry, remorse, and morbid reflection that I may be of service to others. Amen.

When I retire at night...   /   /

Chronology of today's events:

Was I resentful?
    1. Who/what   *3. Affects*

    2. Cause   *4. My part*

Was I selfish?

Was I dishonest?

Was I afraid?

Do I owe an apology?

What have I wrongly kept secret?

Was I kind and loving toward all?

What could I have done better?

How did faith or fear rule my actions today?

Today I gave of my time ___, talent ___, treasure ___, and touch ___.

Who did I help today?

What am I grateful for today?

Who needs my prayers today?

God, forgive me where I have been resentful, selfish, dishonest, or afraid today. Help me not to keep anything to myself, but to discuss it openly with another person. Show me where I owe an apology and help me make it, and help me to be kind and loving to all people. Use me in the mainstream of life, and remove worry, remorse, and morbid reflection that I may be of service to others. Amen.

When I retire at night...   /   /

Chronology of today's events:

Was I resentful?
    1. *Who/what*   3. *Affects*

    2. *Cause*   4. *My part*

Was I selfish?

Was I dishonest?

Was I afraid?

Do I owe an apology?

What have I wrongly kept secret?

Was I kind and loving toward all?

What could I have done better?

How did faith or fear rule my actions today?

Today I gave of my time ___, talent ___, treasure ___, and touch ___.

Who did I help today?

What am I grateful for today?

Who needs my prayers today?

God, forgive me where I have been resentful, selfish, dishonest, or afraid today. Help me not to keep anything to myself, but to discuss it openly with another person. Show me where I owe an apology and help me make it, and help me to be kind and loving to all people. Use me in the mainstream of life, and remove worry, remorse, and morbid reflection that I may be of service to others. Amen.

When I retire at night...   /   /

Chronology of today's events:

Was I resentful?
    1. *Who/what*   3. *Affects*

    2. *Cause*   4. *My part*

Was I selfish?

Was I dishonest?

Was I afraid?

Do I owe an apology?

What have I wrongly kept secret?

Was I kind and loving toward all?

What could I have done better?

How did faith or fear rule my actions today?

Today I gave of my time ___, talent ___, treasure ___, and touch ___.

Who did I help today?

What am I grateful for today?

Who needs my prayers today?

God, forgive me where I have been resentful, selfish, dishonest, or afraid today. Help me not to keep anything to myself, but to discuss it openly with another person. Show me where I owe an apology and help me make it, and help me to be kind and loving to all people. Use me in the mainstream of life, and remove worry, remorse, and morbid reflection that I may be of service to others. Amen.

When I retire at night...   /   /

Chronology of today's events:

Was I resentful?
    1. *Who/what*   3. *Affects*

    2. *Cause*   4. *My part*

Was I selfish?

Was I dishonest?

Was I afraid?

Do I owe an apology?

What have I wrongly kept secret?

Was I kind and loving toward all?

What could I have done better?

How did faith or fear rule my actions today?

Today I gave of my time ___, talent ___, treasure ___, and touch ___.

Who did I help today?

What am I grateful for today?

Who needs my prayers today?

God, forgive me where I have been resentful, selfish, dishonest, or afraid today. Help me not to keep anything to myself, but to discuss it openly with another person. Show me where I owe an apology and help me make it, and help me to be kind and loving to all people. Use me in the mainstream of life, and remove worry, remorse, and morbid reflection that I may be of service to others. Amen.

When I retire at night...   /   /

Chronology of today's events:

Was I resentful?
    1. *Who/what*   3.   *Affects*

    2. *Cause*   4.   *My part*

Was I selfish?

Was I dishonest?

Was I afraid?

Do I owe an apology?

What have I wrongly kept secret?

Was I kind and loving toward all?

What could I have done better?

How did faith or fear rule my actions today?

Today I gave of my time ___, talent ___, treasure ___, and touch ___.

Who did I help today?

What am I grateful for today?

Who needs my prayers today?

God, forgive me where I have been resentful, selfish, dishonest, or afraid today. Help me not to keep anything to myself, but to discuss it openly with another person. Show me where I owe an apology and help me make it, and help me to be kind and loving to all people. Use me in the mainstream of life, and remove worry, remorse, and morbid reflection that I may be of service to others. Amen.

When I retire at night...   /   /

Chronology of today's events:

Was I resentful?
    1. *Who/what*   3. *Affects*

    2. *Cause*   4. *My part*

Was I selfish?

Was I dishonest?

Was I afraid?

Do I owe an apology?

What have I wrongly kept secret?

Was I kind and loving toward all?

What could I have done better?

How did faith or fear rule my actions today?

Today I gave of my time ___, talent ___, treasure ___, and touch ___.

Who did I help today?

What am I grateful for today?

Who needs my prayers today?

God, forgive me where I have been resentful, selfish, dishonest, or afraid today. Help me not to keep anything to myself, but to discuss it openly with another person. Show me where I owe an apology and help me make it, and help me to be kind and loving to all people. Use me in the mainstream of life, and remove worry, remorse, and morbid reflection that I may be of service to others. Amen.

When I retire at night...   /   /

Chronology of today's events:

Was I resentful?
    1. *Who/what*   3. *Affects*

    2. *Cause*   4. *My part*

Was I selfish?

Was I dishonest?

Was I afraid?

Do I owe an apology?

What have I wrongly kept secret?

Was I kind and loving toward all?

What could I have done better?

How did faith or fear rule my actions today?

Today I gave of my time ___, talent ___, treasure ___, and touch ___.

Who did I help today?

What am I grateful for today?

Who needs my prayers today?

God, forgive me where I have been resentful, selfish, dishonest, or afraid today. Help me not to keep anything to myself, but to discuss it openly with another person. Show me where I owe an apology and help me make it, and help me to be kind and loving to all people. Use me in the mainstream of life, and remove worry, remorse, and morbid reflection that I may be of service to others. Amen.

When I retire at night...   /   /

Chronology of today's events:

Was I resentful?
    1. *Who/what*   3. *Affects*

    2. *Cause*   4. *My part*

Was I selfish?

Was I dishonest?

Was I afraid?

Do I owe an apology?

What have I wrongly kept secret?

Was I kind and loving toward all?

What could I have done better?

How did faith or fear rule my actions today?

Today I gave of my time ___, talent ___, treasure ___, and touch ___.

Who did I help today?

What am I grateful for today?

Who needs my prayers today?

God, forgive me where I have been resentful, selfish, dishonest, or afraid today. Help me not to keep anything to myself, but to discuss it openly with another person. Show me where I owe an apology and help me make it, and help me to be kind and loving to all people. Use me in the mainstream of life, and remove worry, remorse, and morbid reflection that I may be of service to others. Amen.

When I retire at night...   /   /

Chronology of today's events:

Was I resentful?
    1. *Who/what*   3. *Affects*

    2. *Cause*   4. *My part*

Was I selfish?

Was I dishonest?

Was I afraid?

Do I owe an apology?

What have I wrongly kept secret?

Was I kind and loving toward all?

What could I have done better?

How did faith or fear rule my actions today?

Today I gave of my time ___, talent ___, treasure ___, and touch ___.

Who did I help today?

What am I grateful for today?

Who needs my prayers today?

God, forgive me where I have been resentful, selfish, dishonest, or afraid today. Help me not to keep anything to myself, but to discuss it openly with another person. Show me where I owe an apology and help me make it, and help me to be kind and loving to all people. Use me in the mainstream of life, and remove worry, remorse, and morbid reflection that I may be of service to others. Amen.

When I retire at night...   /   /

Chronology of today's events:

Was I resentful?
    1. Who/what   *3. Affects*

    2. Cause   *4. My part*

Was I selfish?

Was I dishonest?

Was I afraid?

Do I owe an apology?

What have I wrongly kept secret?

Was I kind and loving toward all?

What could I have done better?

How did faith or fear rule my actions today?

Today I gave of my time ___, talent ___, treasure ___, and touch ___.

Who did I help today?

What am I grateful for today?

Who needs my prayers today?

God, forgive me where I have been resentful, selfish, dishonest, or afraid today. Help me not to keep anything to myself, but to discuss it openly with another person. Show me where I owe an apology and help me make it, and help me to be kind and loving to all people. Use me in the mainstream of life, and remove worry, remorse, and morbid reflection that I may be of service to others. Amen.

When I retire at night...   /   /

Chronology of today's events:

Was I resentful?
    1. Who/what   3. Affects

    2. Cause   4. My part

Was I selfish?

Was I dishonest?

Was I afraid?

Do I owe an apology?

What have I wrongly kept secret?

Was I kind and loving toward all?

What could I have done better?

How did faith or fear rule my actions today?

Today I gave of my time ___, talent ___, treasure ___, and touch ___.

Who did I help today?

What am I grateful for today?

Who needs my prayers today?

God, forgive me where I have been resentful, selfish, dishonest, or afraid today. Help me not to keep anything to myself, but to discuss it openly with another person. Show me where I owe an apology and help me make it, and help me to be kind and loving to all people. Use me in the mainstream of life, and remove worry, remorse, and morbid reflection that I may be of service to others. Amen.

When I retire at night...   /   /

Chronology of today's events:

Was I resentful?
    1. *Who/what*   3. *Affects*

    2. *Cause*   4. *My part*

Was I selfish?

Was I dishonest?

Was I afraid?

Do I owe an apology?

What have I wrongly kept secret?

Was I kind and loving toward all?

What could I have done better?

How did faith or fear rule my actions today?

Today I gave of my time ___, talent ___, treasure ___, and touch ___.

Who did I help today?

What am I grateful for today?

Who needs my prayers today?

God, forgive me where I have been resentful, selfish, dishonest, or afraid today. Help me not to keep anything to myself, but to discuss it openly with another person. Show me where I owe an apology and help me make it, and help me to be kind and loving to all people. Use me in the mainstream of life, and remove worry, remorse, and morbid reflection that I may be of service to others. Amen.

When I retire at night...   /   /

Chronology of today's events:

Was I resentful?
    1. *Who/what*   3. *Affects*

    2. *Cause*   4. *My part*

Was I selfish?

Was I dishonest?

Was I afraid?

Do I owe an apology?

What have I wrongly kept secret?

Was I kind and loving toward all?

What could I have done better?

How did faith or fear rule my actions today?

Today I gave of my time ___, talent ___, treasure ___, and touch ___.

Who did I help today?

What am I grateful for today?

Who needs my prayers today?

God, forgive me where I have been resentful, selfish, dishonest, or afraid today. Help me not to keep anything to myself, but to discuss it openly with another person. Show me where I owe an apology and help me make it, and help me to be kind and loving to all people. Use me in the mainstream of life, and remove worry, remorse, and morbid reflection that I may be of service to others. Amen.

When I retire at night...   /   /

Chronology of today's events:

Was I resentful?
    1. *Who/what*   3. *Affects*

    2. *Cause*   4. *My part*

Was I selfish?

Was I dishonest?

Was I afraid?

Do I owe an apology?

What have I wrongly kept secret?

Was I kind and loving toward all?

What could I have done better?

How did faith or fear rule my actions today?

Today I gave of my time ___, talent ___, treasure ___, and touch ___.

Who did I help today?

What am I grateful for today?

Who needs my prayers today?

God, forgive me where I have been resentful, selfish, dishonest, or afraid today. Help me not to keep anything to myself, but to discuss it openly with another person. Show me where I owe an apology and help me make it, and help me to be kind and loving to all people. Use me in the mainstream of life, and remove worry, remorse, and morbid reflection that I may be of service to others. Amen.

When I retire at night...   /   /

Chronology of today's events:

Was I resentful?
    1. *Who/what*   3. *Affects*

    2. *Cause*   4. *My part*

Was I selfish?

Was I dishonest?

Was I afraid?

Do I owe an apology?

What have I wrongly kept secret?

Was I kind and loving toward all?

What could I have done better?

How did faith or fear rule my actions today?

Today I gave of my time ___, talent ___, treasure ___, and touch ___.

Who did I help today?

What am I grateful for today?

Who needs my prayers today?

God, forgive me where I have been resentful, selfish, dishonest, or afraid today. Help me not to keep anything to myself, but to discuss it openly with another person. Show me where I owe an apology and help me make it, and help me to be kind and loving to all people. Use me in the mainstream of life, and remove worry, remorse, and morbid reflection that I may be of service to others. Amen.

When I retire at night...   /   /

Chronology of today's events:

Was I resentful?
    1. *Who / what*   3. *Affects*

    2. *Cause*   4. *My part*

Was I selfish?

Was I dishonest?

Was I afraid?

Do I owe an apology?

What have I wrongly kept secret?

Was I kind and loving toward all?

What could I have done better?

How did faith or fear rule my actions today?

Today I gave of my time ___, talent ___, treasure ___, and touch ___.

Who did I help today?

What am I grateful for today?

Who needs my prayers today?

God, forgive me where I have been resentful, selfish, dishonest, or afraid today. Help me not to keep anything to myself, but to discuss it openly with another person. Show me where I owe an apology and help me make it, and help me to be kind and loving to all people. Use me in the mainstream of life, and remove worry, remorse, and morbid reflection that I may be of service to others. Amen.

When I retire at night...   /   /

Chronology of today's events:

Was I resentful?
    1. Who/what   3.   Affects

    2. Cause   4.   My part

Was I selfish?

Was I dishonest?

Was I afraid?

Do I owe an apology?

What have I wrongly kept secret?

Was I kind and loving toward all?

What could I have done better?

How did faith or fear rule my actions today?

Today I gave of my time ___, talent ___, treasure ___, and touch ___.

Who did I help today?

What am I grateful for today?

Who needs my prayers today?

God, forgive me where I have been resentful, selfish, dishonest, or afraid today. Help me not to keep anything to myself, but to discuss it openly with another person. Show me where I owe an apology and help me make it, and help me to be kind and loving to all people. Use me in the mainstream of life, and remove worry, remorse, and morbid reflection that I may be of service to others. Amen.

When I retire at night...   /   /

Chronology of today's events:

Was I resentful?
    1. *Who/what*   3. *Affects*

    2. *Cause*   4. *My part*

Was I selfish?

Was I dishonest?

Was I afraid?

Do I owe an apology?

What have I wrongly kept secret?

Was I kind and loving toward all?

What could I have done better?

How did faith or fear rule my actions today?

Today I gave of my time ___, talent ___, treasure ___, and touch ___.

Who did I help today?

What am I grateful for today?

Who needs my prayers today?

God, forgive me where I have been resentful, selfish, dishonest, or afraid today. Help me not to keep anything to myself, but to discuss it openly with another person. Show me where I owe an apology and help me make it, and help me to be kind and loving to all people. Use me in the mainstream of life, and remove worry, remorse, and morbid reflection that I may be of service to others. Amen.

When I retire at night…   /   /

Chronology of today's events:

Was I resentful?
    1. *Who/what*   3. *Affects*

    2. *Cause*   4. *My part*

Was I selfish?

Was I dishonest?

Was I afraid?

Do I owe an apology?

What have I wrongly kept secret?

Was I kind and loving toward all?

What could I have done better?

How did faith or fear rule my actions today?

Today I gave of my time ___, talent ___, treasure ___, and touch ___.

Who did I help today?

What am I grateful for today?

Who needs my prayers today?

God, forgive me where I have been resentful, selfish, dishonest, or afraid today. Help me not to keep anything to myself, but to discuss it openly with another person. Show me where I owe an apology and help me make it, and help me to be kind and loving to all people. Use me in the mainstream of life, and remove worry, remorse, and morbid reflection that I may be of service to others. Amen.

When I retire at night...   /   /

Chronology of today's events:

Was I resentful?
    1. *Who/what*　　　　　　　3. *Affects*

    2. *Cause*　　　　　　　　　4. *My part*

Was I selfish?

Was I dishonest?

Was I afraid?

Do I owe an apology?

What have I wrongly kept secret?

Was I kind and loving toward all?

What could I have done better?

How did faith or fear rule my actions today?

Today I gave of my time ___, talent ___, treasure ___, and touch ___.

Who did I help today?

What am I grateful for today?

Who needs my prayers today?

God, forgive me where I have been resentful, selfish, dishonest, or afraid today. Help me not to keep anything to myself, but to discuss it openly with another person. Show me where I owe an apology and help me make it, and help me to be kind and loving to all people. Use me in the mainstream of life, and remove worry, remorse, and morbid reflection that I may be of service to others. Amen.

When I retire at night...   /   /

Chronology of today's events:

Was I resentful?
    1. *Who/what*   3. *Affects*

    2. *Cause*   4. *My part*

Was I selfish?

Was I dishonest?

Was I afraid?

Do I owe an apology?

What have I wrongly kept secret?

Was I kind and loving toward all?

What could I have done better?

How did faith or fear rule my actions today?

Today I gave of my time ___, talent ___, treasure ___, and touch ___.

Who did I help today?

What am I grateful for today?

Who needs my prayers today?

God, forgive me where I have been resentful, selfish, dishonest, or afraid today. Help me not to keep anything to myself, but to discuss it openly with another person. Show me where I owe an apology and help me make it, and help me to be kind and loving to all people. Use me in the mainstream of life, and remove worry, remorse, and morbid reflection that I may be of service to others. Amen.

When I retire at night...   /   /

Chronology of today's events:

Was I resentful?
    1. *Who / what*   3. *Affects*
    2. *Cause*   4. *My part*

Was I selfish?

Was I dishonest?

Was I afraid?

Do I owe an apology?

What have I wrongly kept secret?

Was I kind and loving toward all?

What could I have done better?

How did faith or fear rule my actions today?

Today I gave of my time ___, talent ___, treasure ___, and touch ___.

Who did I help today?

What am I grateful for today?

Who needs my prayers today?

God, forgive me where I have been resentful, selfish, dishonest, or afraid today. Help me not to keep anything to myself, but to discuss it openly with another person. Show me where I owe an apology and help me make it, and help me to be kind and loving to all people. Use me in the mainstream of life, and remove worry, remorse, and morbid reflection that I may be of service to others. Amen.

When I retire at night...   /   /

Chronology of today's events:

Was I resentful?
    1. Who/what   3.   Affects

    2. Cause   4.   My part

Was I selfish?

Was I dishonest?

Was I afraid?

Do I owe an apology?

What have I wrongly kept secret?

Was I kind and loving toward all?

What could I have done better?

How did faith or fear rule my actions today?

Today I gave of my time ___, talent ___, treasure ___, and touch ___.

Who did I help today?

What am I grateful for today?

Who needs my prayers today?

God, forgive me where I have been resentful, selfish, dishonest, or afraid today. Help me not to keep anything to myself, but to discuss it openly with another person. Show me where I owe an apology and help me make it, and help me to be kind and loving to all people. Use me in the mainstream of life, and remove worry, remorse, and morbid reflection that I may be of service to others. Amen.

When I retire at night...   /   /

Chronology of today's events:

Was I resentful?

    1. Who/what   3. Affects

    2. Cause   4. My part

Was I selfish?

Was I dishonest?

Was I afraid?

Do I owe an apology?

What have I wrongly kept secret?

Was I kind and loving toward all?

What could I have done better?

How did faith or fear rule my actions today?

Today I gave of my time ___, talent ___, treasure ___, and touch ___.

Who did I help today?

What am I grateful for today?

Who needs my prayers today?

God, forgive me where I have been resentful, selfish, dishonest, or afraid today. Help me not to keep anything to myself, but to discuss it openly with another person. Show me where I owe an apology and help me make it, and help me to be kind and loving to all people. Use me in the mainstream of life, and remove worry, remorse, and morbid reflection that I may be of service to others. Amen.

When I retire at night...   /   /

Chronology of today's events:

Was I resentful?
    1. *Who/what*
    2. *Cause*
    3. *Affects*
    4. *My part*

Was I selfish?

Was I dishonest?

Was I afraid?

Do I owe an apology?

What have I wrongly kept secret?

Was I kind and loving toward all?

What could I have done better?

How did faith or fear rule my actions today?

Today I gave of my time ___, talent ___, treasure ___, and touch ___.

Who did I help today?

What am I grateful for today?

Who needs my prayers today?

God, forgive me where I have been resentful, selfish, dishonest, or afraid today. Help me not to keep anything to myself, but to discuss it openly with another person. Show me where I owe an apology and help me make it, and help me to be kind and loving to all people. Use me in the mainstream of life, and remove worry, remorse, and morbid reflection that I may be of service to others. Amen.

When I retire at night...   /   /

Chronology of today's events:

Was I resentful?
    1. *Who/what*   3. *Affects*

    2. *Cause*   4. *My part*

Was I selfish?

Was I dishonest?

Was I afraid?

Do I owe an apology?

What have I wrongly kept secret?

Was I kind and loving toward all?

What could I have done better?

How did faith or fear rule my actions today?

Today I gave of my time ___, talent ___, treasure ___, and touch ___.

Who did I help today?

What am I grateful for today?

Who needs my prayers today?

God, forgive me where I have been resentful, selfish, dishonest, or afraid today. Help me not to keep anything to myself, but to discuss it openly with another person. Show me where I owe an apology and help me make it, and help me to be kind and loving to all people. Use me in the mainstream of life, and remove worry, remorse, and morbid reflection that I may be of service to others. Amen.

When I retire at night...   /   /

Chronology of today's events:

Was I resentful?
    1. *Who/what*   3. *Affects*

    2. *Cause*   4. *My part*

Was I selfish?

Was I dishonest?

Was I afraid?

Do I owe an apology?

What have I wrongly kept secret?

Was I kind and loving toward all?

What could I have done better?

How did faith or fear rule my actions today?

Today I gave of my time ___, talent ___, treasure ___, and touch ___.

Who did I help today?

What am I grateful for today?

Who needs my prayers today?

God, forgive me where I have been resentful, selfish, dishonest, or afraid today. Help me not to keep anything to myself, but to discuss it openly with another person. Show me where I owe an apology and help me make it, and help me to be kind and loving to all people. Use me in the mainstream of life, and remove worry, remorse, and morbid reflection that I may be of service to others. Amen.

When I retire at night...   /   /

Chronology of today's events:

Was I resentful?
   1. *Who/what*   3. *Affects*
   2. *Cause*   4. *My part*

Was I selfish?

Was I dishonest?

Was I afraid?

Do I owe an apology?

What have I wrongly kept secret?

Was I kind and loving toward all?

What could I have done better?

How did faith or fear rule my actions today?

Today I gave of my time ___, talent ___, treasure ___, and touch ___.

Who did I help today?

What am I grateful for today?

Who needs my prayers today?

God, forgive me where I have been resentful, selfish, dishonest, or afraid today. Help me not to keep anything to myself, but to discuss it openly with another person. Show me where I owe an apology and help me make it, and help me to be kind and loving to all people. Use me in the mainstream of life, and remove worry, remorse, and morbid reflection that I may be of service to others. Amen.

When I retire at night...   /   /

Chronology of today's events:

Was I resentful?
    1. Who/what   3. Affects

    2. Cause   4. My part

Was I selfish?

Was I dishonest?

Was I afraid?

Do I owe an apology?

What have I wrongly kept secret?

Was I kind and loving toward all?

What could I have done better?

How did faith or fear rule my actions today?

Today I gave of my time ___, talent ___, treasure ___, and touch ___.

Who did I help today?

What am I grateful for today?

Who needs my prayers today?

God, forgive me where I have been resentful, selfish, dishonest, or afraid today. Help me not to keep anything to myself, but to discuss it openly with another person. Show me where I owe an apology and help me make it, and help me to be kind and loving to all people. Use me in the mainstream of life, and remove worry, remorse, and morbid reflection that I may be of service to others. Amen.

When I retire at night...   /   /

Chronology of today's events:

Was I resentful?

    1. *Who/what*   3. *Affects*

    2. *Cause*   4. *My part*

Was I selfish?

Was I dishonest?

Was I afraid?

Do I owe an apology?

What have I wrongly kept secret?

Was I kind and loving toward all?

What could I have done better?

How did faith or fear rule my actions today?

Today I gave of my time ___, talent ___, treasure ___, and touch ___.

Who did I help today?

What am I grateful for today?

Who needs my prayers today?

God, forgive me where I have been resentful, selfish, dishonest, or afraid today. Help me not to keep anything to myself, but to discuss it openly with another person. Show me where I owe an apology and help me make it, and help me to be kind and loving to all people. Use me in the mainstream of life, and remove worry, remorse, and morbid reflection that I may be of service to others. Amen.

When I retire at night...   /   /

Chronology of today's events:

Was I resentful?
    1. *Who/what*   3. *Affects*

    2. *Cause*   4. *My part*

Was I selfish?

Was I dishonest?

Was I afraid?

Do I owe an apology?

What have I wrongly kept secret?

Was I kind and loving toward all?

What could I have done better?

How did faith or fear rule my actions today?

Today I gave of my time ___, talent ___, treasure ___, and touch ___.

Who did I help today?

What am I grateful for today?

Who needs my prayers today?

God, forgive me where I have been resentful, selfish, dishonest, or afraid today. Help me not to keep anything to myself, but to discuss it openly with another person. Show me where I owe an apology and help me make it, and help me to be kind and loving to all people. Use me in the mainstream of life, and remove worry, remorse, and morbid reflection that I may be of service to others. Amen.

When I retire at night...   /   /

Chronology of today's events:

Was I resentful?
    1. *Who/what*　　　　　　　3. *Affects*

    2. *Cause*　　　　　　　　　4. *My part*

Was I selfish?

Was I dishonest?

Was I afraid?

Do I owe an apology?

What have I wrongly kept secret?

Was I kind and loving toward all?

What could I have done better?

How did faith or fear rule my actions today?

Today I gave of my time ___, talent ___, treasure ___, and touch ___.

Who did I help today?

What am I grateful for today?

Who needs my prayers today?

God, forgive me where I have been resentful, selfish, dishonest, or afraid today. Help me not to keep anything to myself, but to discuss it openly with another person. Show me where I owe an apology and help me make it, and help me to be kind and loving to all people. Use me in the mainstream of life, and remove worry, remorse, and morbid reflection that I may be of service to others. Amen.

When I retire at night…   /   /

Chronology of today's events:

Was I resentful?

    1. *Who/what*   3. *Affects*

    2. *Cause*   4. *My part*

Was I selfish?

Was I dishonest?

Was I afraid?

Do I owe an apology?

What have I wrongly kept secret?

Was I kind and loving toward all?

What could I have done better?

How did faith or fear rule my actions today?

Today I gave of my time ___, talent ___, treasure ___, and touch ___.

Who did I help today?

What am I grateful for today?

Who needs my prayers today?

God, forgive me where I have been resentful, selfish, dishonest, or afraid today. Help me not to keep anything to myself, but to discuss it openly with another person. Show me where I owe an apology and help me make it, and help me to be kind and loving to all people. Use me in the mainstream of life, and remove worry, remorse, and morbid reflection that I may be of service to others. Amen.

When I retire at night...   /   /

Chronology of today's events:

Was I resentful?
    1. *Who/what*
    2. *Cause*
    3. *Affects*
    4. *My part*

Was I selfish?

Was I dishonest?

Was I afraid?

Do I owe an apology?

What have I wrongly kept secret?

Was I kind and loving toward all?

What could I have done better?

How did faith or fear rule my actions today?

Today I gave of my time ___, talent ___, treasure ___, and touch ___.

Who did I help today?

What am I grateful for today?

Who needs my prayers today?

God, forgive me where I have been resentful, selfish, dishonest, or afraid today. Help me not to keep anything to myself, but to discuss it openly with another person. Show me where I owe an apology and help me make it, and help me to be kind and loving to all people. Use me in the mainstream of life, and remove worry, remorse, and morbid reflection that I may be of service to others. Amen.

When I retire at night...   /   /

Chronology of today's events:

Was I resentful?
    1. Who/what   3. Affects

    2. Cause   4. My part

Was I selfish?

Was I dishonest?

Was I afraid?

Do I owe an apology?

What have I wrongly kept secret?

Was I kind and loving toward all?

What could I have done better?

How did faith or fear rule my actions today?

Today I gave of my time ___, talent ___, treasure ___, and touch ___.

Who did I help today?

What am I grateful for today?

Who needs my prayers today?

God, forgive me where I have been resentful, selfish, dishonest, or afraid today. Help me not to keep anything to myself, but to discuss it openly with another person. Show me where I owe an apology and help me make it, and help me to be kind and loving to all people. Use me in the mainstream of life, and remove worry, remorse, and morbid reflection that I may be of service to others. Amen.

When I retire at night...   /   /

Chronology of today's events:

Was I resentful?
    1. Who/what   3. Affects

    2. Cause   4. My part

Was I selfish?

Was I dishonest?

Was I afraid?

Do I owe an apology?

What have I wrongly kept secret?

Was I kind and loving toward all?

What could I have done better?

How did faith or fear rule my actions today?

Today I gave of my time ___, talent ___, treasure ___, and touch ___.

Who did I help today?

What am I grateful for today?

Who needs my prayers today?

God, forgive me where I have been resentful, selfish, dishonest, or afraid today. Help me not to keep anything to myself, but to discuss it openly with another person. Show me where I owe an apology and help me make it, and help me to be kind and loving to all people. Use me in the mainstream of life, and remove worry, remorse, and morbid reflection that I may be of service to others. Amen.

When I retire at night...   /   /

Chronology of today's events:

Was I resentful?
    1. *Who/what*   3. *Affects*

    2. *Cause*   4. *My part*

Was I selfish?

Was I dishonest?

Was I afraid?

Do I owe an apology?

What have I wrongly kept secret?

Was I kind and loving toward all?

What could I have done better?

How did faith or fear rule my actions today?

Today I gave of my time ___, talent ___, treasure ___, and touch ___.

Who did I help today?

What am I grateful for today?

Who needs my prayers today?

God, forgive me where I have been resentful, selfish, dishonest, or afraid today. Help me not to keep anything to myself, but to discuss it openly with another person. Show me where I owe an apology and help me make it, and help me to be kind and loving to all people. Use me in the mainstream of life, and remove worry, remorse, and morbid reflection that I may be of service to others. Amen.

When I retire at night...   /   /

Chronology of today's events:

Was I resentful?
   1. *Who/what*   3. *Affects*

   2. *Cause*   4. *My part*

Was I selfish?

Was I dishonest?

Was I afraid?

Do I owe an apology?

What have I wrongly kept secret?

Was I kind and loving toward all?

What could I have done better?

How did faith or fear rule my actions today?

Today I gave of my time ___, talent ___, treasure ___, and touch ___.

Who did I help today?

What am I grateful for today?

Who needs my prayers today?

God, forgive me where I have been resentful, selfish, dishonest, or afraid today. Help me not to keep anything to myself, but to discuss it openly with another person. Show me where I owe an apology and help me make it, and help me to be kind and loving to all people. Use me in the mainstream of life, and remove worry, remorse, and morbid reflection that I may be of service to others. Amen.

When I retire at night...   /   /

Chronology of today's events:

Was I resentful?
    1. *Who/what*   3. *Affects*

    2. *Cause*   4. *My part*

Was I selfish?

Was I dishonest?

Was I afraid?

Do I owe an apology?

What have I wrongly kept secret?

Was I kind and loving toward all?

What could I have done better?

How did faith or fear rule my actions today?

Today I gave of my time ___, talent ___, treasure ___, and touch ___.

Who did I help today?

What am I grateful for today?

Who needs my prayers today?

God, forgive me where I have been resentful, selfish, dishonest, or afraid today. Help me not to keep anything to myself, but to discuss it openly with another person. Show me where I owe an apology and help me make it, and help me to be kind and loving to all people. Use me in the mainstream of life, and remove worry, remorse, and morbid reflection that I may be of service to others. Amen.

When I retire at night...   /   /

Chronology of today's events:

Was I resentful?
    1. *Who/what*   3. *Affects*

    2. *Cause*   4. *My part*

Was I selfish?

Was I dishonest?

Was I afraid?

Do I owe an apology?

What have I wrongly kept secret?

Was I kind and loving toward all?

What could I have done better?

How did faith or fear rule my actions today?

Today I gave of my time ___, talent ___, treasure ___, and touch ___.

Who did I help today?

What am I grateful for today?

Who needs my prayers today?

God, forgive me where I have been resentful, selfish, dishonest, or afraid today. Help me not to keep anything to myself, but to discuss it openly with another person. Show me where I owe an apology and help me make it, and help me to be kind and loving to all people. Use me in the mainstream of life, and remove worry, remorse, and morbid reflection that I may be of service to others. Amen.

When I retire at night...   /   /

Chronology of today's events:

Was I resentful?
    1. Who/what   3. Affects

    2. Cause   4. My part

Was I selfish?

Was I dishonest?

Was I afraid?

Do I owe an apology?

What have I wrongly kept secret?

Was I kind and loving toward all?

What could I have done better?

How did faith or fear rule my actions today?

Today I gave of my time ____, talent ____, treasure ____, and touch ____.

Who did I help today?

What am I grateful for today?

Who needs my prayers today?

God, forgive me where I have been resentful, selfish, dishonest, or afraid today. Help me not to keep anything to myself, but to discuss it openly with another person. Show me where I owe an apology and help me make it, and help me to be kind and loving to all people. Use me in the mainstream of life, and remove worry, remorse, and morbid reflection that I may be of service to others. Amen.

When I retire at night...   /   /

Chronology of today's events:

Was I resentful?
  1. Who/what   3. Affects
  2. Cause   4. My part

Was I selfish?

Was I dishonest?

Was I afraid?

Do I owe an apology?

What have I wrongly kept secret?

Was I kind and loving toward all?

What could I have done better?

How did faith or fear rule my actions today?

Today I gave of my time ___, talent ___, treasure ___, and touch ___.

Who did I help today?

What am I grateful for today?

Who needs my prayers today?

God, forgive me where I have been resentful, selfish, dishonest, or afraid today. Help me not to keep anything to myself, but to discuss it openly with another person. Show me where I owe an apology and help me make it, and help me to be kind and loving to all people. Use me in the mainstream of life, and remove worry, remorse, and morbid reflection that I may be of service to others. Amen.

When I retire at night...   /   /

Chronology of today's events:

Was I resentful?
    1. *Who/what*   3. *Affects*

    2. *Cause*   4. *My part*

Was I selfish?

Was I dishonest?

Was I afraid?

Do I owe an apology?

What have I wrongly kept secret?

Was I kind and loving toward all?

What could I have done better?

How did faith or fear rule my actions today?

Today I gave of my time ___, talent ___, treasure ___, and touch ___.

Who did I help today?

What am I grateful for today?

Who needs my prayers today?

God, forgive me where I have been resentful, selfish, dishonest, or afraid today. Help me not to keep anything to myself, but to discuss it openly with another person. Show me where I owe an apology and help me make it, and help me to be kind and loving to all people. Use me in the mainstream of life, and remove worry, remorse, and morbid reflection that I may be of service to others. Amen.

When I retire at night...   /   /

Chronology of today's events:

Was I resentful?
    1. *Who/what*　　　　　　　3. *Affects*

    2. *Cause*　　　　　　　　　4. *My part*

Was I selfish?

Was I dishonest?

Was I afraid?

Do I owe an apology?

What have I wrongly kept secret?

Was I kind and loving toward all?

What could I have done better?

How did faith or fear rule my actions today?

Today I gave of my time ___, talent ___, treasure ___, and touch ___.

Who did I help today?

What am I grateful for today?

Who needs my prayers today?

God, forgive me where I have been resentful, selfish, dishonest, or afraid today. Help me not to keep anything to myself, but to discuss it openly with another person. Show me where I owe an apology and help me make it, and help me to be kind and loving to all people. Use me in the mainstream of life, and remove worry, remorse, and morbid reflection that I may be of service to others. Amen.

When I retire at night...   /   /

Chronology of today's events:

Was I resentful?
   1. *Who/what*   3. *Affects*
   2. *Cause*   4. *My part*

Was I selfish?

Was I dishonest?

Was I afraid?

Do I owe an apology?

What have I wrongly kept secret?

Was I kind and loving toward all?

What could I have done better?

How did faith or fear rule my actions today?

Today I gave of my time ___, talent ___, treasure ___, and touch ___.

Who did I help today?

What am I grateful for today?

Who needs my prayers today?

God, forgive me where I have been resentful, selfish, dishonest, or afraid today. Help me not to keep anything to myself, but to discuss it openly with another person. Show me where I owe an apology and help me make it, and help me to be kind and loving to all people. Use me in the mainstream of life, and remove worry, remorse, and morbid reflection that I may be of service to others. Amen.

When I retire at night…   /   /

Chronology of today's events:

_____
_____
_____

Was I resentful?
    1. *Who/what*   3. *Affects*

    2. *Cause*   4. *My part*

Was I selfish?

Was I dishonest?

Was I afraid?

Do I owe an apology?

What have I wrongly kept secret?

Was I kind and loving toward all?

What could I have done better?

How did faith or fear rule my actions today?

Today I gave of my time ___, talent ___, treasure ___, and touch ___.

Who did I help today?

What am I grateful for today?

Who needs my prayers today?

God, forgive me where I have been resentful, selfish, dishonest, or afraid today. Help me not to keep anything to myself, but to discuss it openly with another person. Show me where I owe an apology and help me make it, and help me to be kind and loving to all people. Use me in the mainstream of life, and remove worry, remorse, and morbid reflection that I may be of service to others. Amen.

When I retire at night...   /   /

Chronology of today's events:

Was I resentful?
    1. Who/what   3. Affects

    2. Cause   4. My part

Was I selfish?

Was I dishonest?

Was I afraid?

Do I owe an apology?

What have I wrongly kept secret?

Was I kind and loving toward all?

What could I have done better?

How did faith or fear rule my actions today?

Today I gave of my time ___, talent ___, treasure ___, and touch ___.

Who did I help today?

What am I grateful for today?

Who needs my prayers today?

God, forgive me where I have been resentful, selfish, dishonest, or afraid today. Help me not to keep anything to myself, but to discuss it openly with another person. Show me where I owe an apology and help me make it, and help me to be kind and loving to all people. Use me in the mainstream of life, and remove worry, remorse, and morbid reflection that I may be of service to others. Amen.

When I retire at night...   /   /

Chronology of today's events:

Was I resentful?
    1. Who/what   3. Affects

    2. Cause   4. My part

Was I selfish?

Was I dishonest?

Was I afraid?

Do I owe an apology?

What have I wrongly kept secret?

Was I kind and loving toward all?

What could I have done better?

How did faith or fear rule my actions today?

Today I gave of my time ___, talent ___, treasure ___, and touch ___.

Who did I help today?

What am I grateful for today?

Who needs my prayers today?

God, forgive me where I have been resentful, selfish, dishonest, or afraid today. Help me not to keep anything to myself, but to discuss it openly with another person. Show me where I owe an apology and help me make it, and help me to be kind and loving to all people. Use me in the mainstream of life, and remove worry, remorse, and morbid reflection that I may be of service to others. Amen.

When I retire at night...   /   /

Chronology of today's events:

Was I resentful?
    1. *Who/what*　　　　　　3. *Affects*

    2. *Cause*　　　　　　　　4. *My part*

Was I selfish?

Was I dishonest?

Was I afraid?

Do I owe an apology?

What have I wrongly kept secret?

Was I kind and loving toward all?

What could I have done better?

How did faith or fear rule my actions today?

Today I gave of my time ___, talent ___, treasure ___, and touch ___.

Who did I help today?

What am I grateful for today?

Who needs my prayers today?

God, forgive me where I have been resentful, selfish, dishonest, or afraid today. Help me not to keep anything to myself, but to discuss it openly with another person. Show me where I owe an apology and help me make it, and help me to be kind and loving to all people. Use me in the mainstream of life, and remove worry, remorse, and morbid reflection that I may be of service to others. Amen.

When I retire at night...   /   /

Chronology of today's events:

Was I resentful?
    1. *Who/what*   3.   *Affects*

    2. *Cause*   4.   *My part*

Was I selfish?

Was I dishonest?

Was I afraid?

Do I owe an apology?

What have I wrongly kept secret?

Was I kind and loving toward all?

What could I have done better?

How did faith or fear rule my actions today?

Today I gave of my time ___, talent ___, treasure ___, and touch ___.

Who did I help today?

What am I grateful for today?

Who needs my prayers today?

God, forgive me where I have been resentful, selfish, dishonest, or afraid today. Help me not to keep anything to myself, but to discuss it openly with another person. Show me where I owe an apology and help me make it, and help me to be kind and loving to all people. Use me in the mainstream of life, and remove worry, remorse, and morbid reflection that I may be of service to others. Amen.

When I retire at night...   /   /

Chronology of today's events:

Was I resentful?
   1. *Who/what*　　　　　　　3. *Affects*

   2. *Cause*　　　　　　　　　4. *My part*

Was I selfish?

Was I dishonest?

Was I afraid?

Do I owe an apology?

What have I wrongly kept secret?

Was I kind and loving toward all?

What could I have done better?

How did faith or fear rule my actions today?

Today I gave of my time ___, talent ___, treasure ___, and touch ___.

Who did I help today?

What am I grateful for today?

Who needs my prayers today?

God, forgive me where I have been resentful, selfish, dishonest, or afraid today. Help me not to keep anything to myself, but to discuss it openly with another person. Show me where I owe an apology and help me make it, and help me to be kind and loving to all people. Use me in the mainstream of life, and remove worry, remorse, and morbid reflection that I may be of service to others. Amen.

When I retire at night...   /   /

Chronology of today's events:

Was I resentful?
- 1. *Who/what*
- 2. *Cause*
- 3. *Affects*
- 4. *My part*

Was I selfish?

Was I dishonest?

Was I afraid?

Do I owe an apology?

What have I wrongly kept secret?

Was I kind and loving toward all?

What could I have done better?

How did faith or fear rule my actions today?

Today I gave of my time ___, talent ___, treasure ___, and touch ___.

Who did I help today?

What am I grateful for today?

Who needs my prayers today?

God, forgive me where I have been resentful, selfish, dishonest, or afraid today. Help me not to keep anything to myself, but to discuss it openly with another person. Show me where I owe an apology and help me make it, and help me to be kind and loving to all people. Use me in the mainstream of life, and remove worry, remorse, and morbid reflection that I may be of service to others. Amen.

When I retire at night...   /   /

Chronology of today's events:

Was I resentful?
   1. *Who/what*   3. *Affects*

   2. *Cause*   4. *My part*

Was I selfish?

Was I dishonest?

Was I afraid?

Do I owe an apology?

What have I wrongly kept secret?

Was I kind and loving toward all?

What could I have done better?

How did faith or fear rule my actions today?

Today I gave of my time ___, talent ___, treasure ___, and touch ___.

Who did I help today?

What am I grateful for today?

Who needs my prayers today?

God, forgive me where I have been resentful, selfish, dishonest, or afraid today. Help me not to keep anything to myself, but to discuss it openly with another person. Show me where I owe an apology and help me make it, and help me to be kind and loving to all people. Use me in the mainstream of life, and remove worry, remorse, and morbid reflection that I may be of service to others. Amen.

When I retire at night...   /   /

Chronology of today's events:

Was I resentful?
    1. Who/what   3. Affects

    2. Cause   4. My part

Was I selfish?

Was I dishonest?

Was I afraid?

Do I owe an apology?

What have I wrongly kept secret?

Was I kind and loving toward all?

What could I have done better?

How did faith or fear rule my actions today?

Today I gave of my time ___, talent ___, treasure ___, and touch ___.

Who did I help today?

What am I grateful for today?

Who needs my prayers today?

God, forgive me where I have been resentful, selfish, dishonest, or afraid today. Help me not to keep anything to myself, but to discuss it openly with another person. Show me where I owe an apology and help me make it, and help me to be kind and loving to all people. Use me in the mainstream of life, and remove worry, remorse, and morbid reflection that I may be of service to others. Amen.

When I retire at night... / /

Chronology of today's events:

Was I resentful?
    1. *Who/what*   3. *Affects*

    2. *Cause*   4. *My part*

Was I selfish?

Was I dishonest?

Was I afraid?

Do I owe an apology?

What have I wrongly kept secret?

Was I kind and loving toward all?

What could I have done better?

How did faith or fear rule my actions today?

Today I gave of my time ___, talent ___, treasure ___, and touch ___.

Who did I help today?

What am I grateful for today?

Who needs my prayers today?

God, forgive me where I have been resentful, selfish, dishonest, or afraid today. Help me not to keep anything to myself, but to discuss it openly with another person. Show me where I owe an apology and help me make it, and help me to be kind and loving to all people. Use me in the mainstream of life, and remove worry, remorse, and morbid reflection that I may be of service to others. Amen.

When I retire at night...   /   /

Chronology of today's events:

Was I resentful?
    1. *Who/what*   3. *Affects*

    2. *Cause*   4. *My part*

Was I selfish?

Was I dishonest?

Was I afraid?

Do I owe an apology?

What have I wrongly kept secret?

Was I kind and loving toward all?

What could I have done better?

How did faith or fear rule my actions today?

Today I gave of my time ___, talent ___, treasure ___, and touch ___.

Who did I help today?

What am I grateful for today?

Who needs my prayers today?

God, forgive me where I have been resentful, selfish, dishonest, or afraid today. Help me not to keep anything to myself, but to discuss it openly with another person. Show me where I owe an apology and help me make it, and help me to be kind and loving to all people. Use me in the mainstream of life, and remove worry, remorse, and morbid reflection that I may be of service to others. Amen.

When I retire at night...   /   /

Chronology of today's events:

Was I resentful?
    1. *Who/what*   3. *Affects*

    2. *Cause*   4. *My part*

Was I selfish?

Was I dishonest?

Was I afraid?

Do I owe an apology?

What have I wrongly kept secret?

Was I kind and loving toward all?

What could I have done better?

How did faith or fear rule my actions today?

Today I gave of my time ___, talent ___, treasure ___, and touch ___.

Who did I help today?

What am I grateful for today?

Who needs my prayers today?

God, forgive me where I have been resentful, selfish, dishonest, or afraid today. Help me not to keep anything to myself, but to discuss it openly with another person. Show me where I owe an apology and help me make it, and help me to be kind and loving to all people. Use me in the mainstream of life, and remove worry, remorse, and morbid reflection that I may be of service to others. Amen.

When I retire at night...   /   /

Chronology of today's events:

Was I resentful?
    1. *Who/what*   3. *Affects*

    2. *Cause*   4. *My part*

Was I selfish?

Was I dishonest?

Was I afraid?

Do I owe an apology?

What have I wrongly kept secret?

Was I kind and loving toward all?

What could I have done better?

How did faith or fear rule my actions today?

Today I gave of my time ___, talent ___, treasure ___, and touch ___.

Who did I help today?

What am I grateful for today?

Who needs my prayers today?

God, forgive me where I have been resentful, selfish, dishonest, or afraid today. Help me not to keep anything to myself, but to discuss it openly with another person. Show me where I owe an apology and help me make it, and help me to be kind and loving to all people. Use me in the mainstream of life, and remove worry, remorse, and morbid reflection that I may be of service to others. Amen.

When I retire at night...   /   /

Chronology of today's events:

Was I resentful?
   1. Who/what   3. Affects

   2. Cause   4. My part

Was I selfish?

Was I dishonest?

Was I afraid?

Do I owe an apology?

What have I wrongly kept secret?

Was I kind and loving toward all?

What could I have done better?

How did faith or fear rule my actions today?

Today I gave of my time ___, talent ___, treasure ___, and touch ___.

Who did I help today?

What am I grateful for today?

Who needs my prayers today?

God, forgive me where I have been resentful, selfish, dishonest, or afraid today. Help me not to keep anything to myself, but to discuss it openly with another person. Show me where I owe an apology and help me make it, and help me to be kind and loving to all people. Use me in the mainstream of life, and remove worry, remorse, and morbid reflection that I may be of service to others. Amen.

When I retire at night...   /   /

Chronology of today's events:

Was I resentful?
   1. Who/what   3. Affects

   2. Cause   4. My part

Was I selfish?

Was I dishonest?

Was I afraid?

Do I owe an apology?

What have I wrongly kept secret?

Was I kind and loving toward all?

What could I have done better?

How did faith or fear rule my actions today?

Today I gave of my time ____, talent ____, treasure ____, and touch ____.

Who did I help today?

What am I grateful for today?

Who needs my prayers today?

God, forgive me where I have been resentful, selfish, dishonest, or afraid today. Help me not to keep anything to myself, but to discuss it openly with another person. Show me where I owe an apology and help me make it, and help me to be kind and loving to all people. Use me in the mainstream of life, and remove worry, remorse, and morbid reflection that I may be of service to others. Amen.

When I retire at night...   /   /

Chronology of today's events:

Was I resentful?
    1. *Who/what*   3.   *Affects*

    2. *Cause*   4.   *My part*

Was I selfish?

Was I dishonest?

Was I afraid?

Do I owe an apology?

What have I wrongly kept secret?

Was I kind and loving toward all?

What could I have done better?

How did faith or fear rule my actions today?

Today I gave of my time ___, talent ___, treasure ___, and touch ___.

Who did I help today?

What am I grateful for today?

Who needs my prayers today?

God, forgive me where I have been resentful, selfish, dishonest, or afraid today. Help me not to keep anything to myself, but to discuss it openly with another person. Show me where I owe an apology and help me make it, and help me to be kind and loving to all people. Use me in the mainstream of life, and remove worry, remorse, and morbid reflection that I may be of service to others. Amen.

When I retire at night...   /   /

Chronology of today's events:

Was I resentful?
    1. *Who/what*   3. *Affects*

    2. *Cause*   4. *My part*

Was I selfish?

Was I dishonest?

Was I afraid?

Do I owe an apology?

What have I wrongly kept secret?

Was I kind and loving toward all?

What could I have done better?

How did faith or fear rule my actions today?

Today I gave of my time ___, talent ___, treasure ___, and touch ___.

Who did I help today?

What am I grateful for today?

Who needs my prayers today?

God, forgive me where I have been resentful, selfish, dishonest, or afraid today. Help me not to keep anything to myself, but to discuss it openly with another person. Show me where I owe an apology and help me make it, and help me to be kind and loving to all people. Use me in the mainstream of life, and remove worry, remorse, and morbid reflection that I may be of service to others. Amen.

When I retire at night...   /   /

Chronology of today's events:

Was I resentful?
    1. *Who/what*　　　　　　　　3. *Affects*

    2. *Cause*　　　　　　　　　　4. *My part*

Was I selfish?

Was I dishonest?

Was I afraid?

Do I owe an apology?

What have I wrongly kept secret?

Was I kind and loving toward all?

What could I have done better?

How did faith or fear rule my actions today?

Today I gave of my time ___, talent ___, treasure ___, and touch ___.

Who did I help today?

What am I grateful for today?

Who needs my prayers today?

God, forgive me where I have been resentful, selfish, dishonest, or afraid today. Help me not to keep anything to myself, but to discuss it openly with another person. Show me where I owe an apology and help me make it, and help me to be kind and loving to all people. Use me in the mainstream of life, and remove worry, remorse, and morbid reflection that I may be of service to others. Amen.

When I retire at night...   /   /

Chronology of today's events:

Was I resentful?
    1. *Who/what*
    2. *Cause*
    3. *Affects*
    4. *My part*

Was I selfish?

Was I dishonest?

Was I afraid?

Do I owe an apology?

What have I wrongly kept secret?

Was I kind and loving toward all?

What could I have done better?

How did faith or fear rule my actions today?

Today I gave of my time ___, talent ___, treasure ___, and touch ___.

Who did I help today?

What am I grateful for today?

Who needs my prayers today?

God, forgive me where I have been resentful, selfish, dishonest, or afraid today. Help me not to keep anything to myself, but to discuss it openly with another person. Show me where I owe an apology and help me make it, and help me to be kind and loving to all people. Use me in the mainstream of life, and remove worry, remorse, and morbid reflection that I may be of service to others. Amen.

When I retire at night...   /   /

Chronology of today's events:

Was I resentful?
    1. Who/what   3. Affects

    2. Cause   4. My part

Was I selfish?

Was I dishonest?

Was I afraid?

Do I owe an apology?

What have I wrongly kept secret?

Was I kind and loving toward all?

What could I have done better?

How did faith or fear rule my actions today?

Today I gave of my time ___, talent ___, treasure ___, and touch ___.

Who did I help today?

What am I grateful for today?

Who needs my prayers today?

God, forgive me where I have been resentful, selfish, dishonest, or afraid today. Help me not to keep anything to myself, but to discuss it openly with another person. Show me where I owe an apology and help me make it, and help me to be kind and loving to all people. Use me in the mainstream of life, and remove worry, remorse, and morbid reflection that I may be of service to others. Amen.

When I retire at night...   /   /

Chronology of today's events:

Was I resentful?
   1. Who/what   3. Affects

   2. Cause   4. My part

Was I selfish?

Was I dishonest?

Was I afraid?

Do I owe an apology?

What have I wrongly kept secret?

Was I kind and loving toward all?

What could I have done better?

How did faith or fear rule my actions today?

Today I gave of my time ___, talent ___, treasure ___, and touch ___.

Who did I help today?

What am I grateful for today?

Who needs my prayers today?

God, forgive me where I have been resentful, selfish, dishonest, or afraid today. Help me not to keep anything to myself, but to discuss it openly with another person. Show me where I owe an apology and help me make it, and help me to be kind and loving to all people. Use me in the mainstream of life, and remove worry, remorse, and morbid reflection that I may be of service to others. Amen.

When I retire at night...   /   /

Chronology of today's events:

Was I resentful?
    1. *Who/what*   3. *Affects*

    2. *Cause*   4. *My part*

Was I selfish?

Was I dishonest?

Was I afraid?

Do I owe an apology?

What have I wrongly kept secret?

Was I kind and loving toward all?

What could I have done better?

How did faith or fear rule my actions today?

Today I gave of my time ___, talent ___, treasure ___, and touch ___.

Who did I help today?

What am I grateful for today?

Who needs my prayers today?

God, forgive me where I have been resentful, selfish, dishonest, or afraid today. Help me not to keep anything to myself, but to discuss it openly with another person. Show me where I owe an apology and help me make it, and help me to be kind and loving to all people. Use me in the mainstream of life, and remove worry, remorse, and morbid reflection that I may be of service to others. Amen.

When I retire at night...   /   /

Chronology of today's events:

_____
_____
_____

Was I resentful?
    1. *Who/what*   3. *Affects*

    2. *Cause*   4. *My part*

Was I selfish?

Was I dishonest?

Was I afraid?

Do I owe an apology?

What have I wrongly kept secret?

Was I kind and loving toward all?

What could I have done better?

How did faith or fear rule my actions today?

Today I gave of my time ___, talent ___, treasure ___, and touch ___.

Who did I help today?

What am I grateful for today?

Who needs my prayers today?

God, forgive me where I have been resentful, selfish, dishonest, or afraid today. Help me not to keep anything to myself, but to discuss it openly with another person. Show me where I owe an apology and help me make it, and help me to be kind and loving to all people. Use me in the mainstream of life, and remove worry, remorse, and morbid reflection that I may be of service to others. Amen.

When I retire at night...   /   /

Chronology of today's events:

Was I resentful?

    1. *Who/what*   3. *Affects*

    2. *Cause*   4. *My part*

Was I selfish?

Was I dishonest?

Was I afraid?

Do I owe an apology?

What have I wrongly kept secret?

Was I kind and loving toward all?

What could I have done better?

How did faith or fear rule my actions today?

Today I gave of my time ___, talent ___, treasure ___, and touch ___.

Who did I help today?

What am I grateful for today?

Who needs my prayers today?

God, forgive me where I have been resentful, selfish, dishonest, or afraid today. Help me not to keep anything to myself, but to discuss it openly with another person. Show me where I owe an apology and help me make it, and help me to be kind and loving to all people. Use me in the mainstream of life, and remove worry, remorse, and morbid reflection that I may be of service to others. Amen.

When I retire at night…   /   /

Chronology of today's events:

Was I resentful?
1. *Who/what*
2. *Cause*
3. *Affects*
4. *My part*

Was I selfish?

Was I dishonest?

Was I afraid?

Do I owe an apology?

What have I wrongly kept secret?

Was I kind and loving toward all?

What could I have done better?

How did faith or fear rule my actions today?

Today I gave of my time ___, talent ___, treasure ___, and touch ___.

Who did I help today?

What am I grateful for today?

Who needs my prayers today?

God, forgive me where I have been resentful, selfish, dishonest, or afraid today. Help me not to keep anything to myself, but to discuss it openly with another person. Show me where I owe an apology and help me make it, and help me to be kind and loving to all people. Use me in the mainstream of life, and remove worry, remorse, and morbid reflection that I may be of service to others. Amen.

When I retire at night…   /   /

Chronology of today's events:

Was I resentful?
    1. Who/what   3. Affects

    2. Cause   4. My part

Was I selfish?

Was I dishonest?

Was I afraid?

Do I owe an apology?

What have I wrongly kept secret?

Was I kind and loving toward all?

What could I have done better?

How did faith or fear rule my actions today?

Today I gave of my time ___, talent ___, treasure ___, and touch ___.

Who did I help today?

What am I grateful for today?

Who needs my prayers today?

God, forgive me where I have been resentful, selfish, dishonest, or afraid today. Help me not to keep anything to myself, but to discuss it openly with another person. Show me where I owe an apology and help me make it, and help me to be kind and loving to all people. Use me in the mainstream of life, and remove worry, remorse, and morbid reflection that I may be of service to others. Amen.

When I retire at night...   /   /

Chronology of today's events:

_____
_____
_____

Was I resentful?
    1. *Who/what*   3. *Affects*

    2. *Cause*   4. *My part*

Was I selfish?

Was I dishonest?

Was I afraid?

Do I owe an apology?

What have I wrongly kept secret?

Was I kind and loving toward all?

What could I have done better?

How did faith or fear rule my actions today?

Today I gave of my time ___, talent ___, treasure ___, and touch ___.

Who did I help today?

What am I grateful for today?

Who needs my prayers today?

God, forgive me where I have been resentful, selfish, dishonest, or afraid today. Help me not to keep anything to myself, but to discuss it openly with another person. Show me where I owe an apology and help me make it, and help me to be kind and loving to all people. Use me in the mainstream of life, and remove worry, remorse, and morbid reflection that I may be of service to others. Amen.

When I retire at night...   /   /

Chronology of today's events:

Was I resentful?
    1. *Who/what*   3. *Affects*

    2. *Cause*   4. *My part*

Was I selfish?

Was I dishonest?

Was I afraid?

Do I owe an apology?

What have I wrongly kept secret?

Was I kind and loving toward all?

What could I have done better?

How did faith or fear rule my actions today?

Today I gave of my time ___, talent ___, treasure ___, and touch ___.

Who did I help today?

What am I grateful for today?

Who needs my prayers today?

God, forgive me where I have been resentful, selfish, dishonest, or afraid today. Help me not to keep anything to myself, but to discuss it openly with another person. Show me where I owe an apology and help me make it, and help me to be kind and loving to all people. Use me in the mainstream of life, and remove worry, remorse, and morbid reflection that I may be of service to others. Amen.

When I retire at night...   /   /

Chronology of today's events:

Was I resentful?
    1. *Who/what*　　　　　　　　3. *Affects*

    2. *Cause*　　　　　　　　　　4. *My part*

Was I selfish?

Was I dishonest?

Was I afraid?

Do I owe an apology?

What have I wrongly kept secret?

Was I kind and loving toward all?

What could I have done better?

How did faith or fear rule my actions today?

Today I gave of my time ___, talent ___, treasure ___, and touch ___.

Who did I help today?

What am I grateful for today?

Who needs my prayers today?

God, forgive me where I have been resentful, selfish, dishonest, or afraid today. Help me not to keep anything to myself, but to discuss it openly with another person. Show me where I owe an apology and help me make it, and help me to be kind and loving to all people. Use me in the mainstream of life, and remove worry, remorse, and morbid reflection that I may be of service to others. Amen.

When I retire at night...   /   /

Chronology of today's events:

Was I resentful?
    1. *Who/what*   3. *Affects*

    2. *Cause*   4. *My part*

Was I selfish?

Was I dishonest?

Was I afraid?

Do I owe an apology?

What have I wrongly kept secret?

Was I kind and loving toward all?

What could I have done better?

How did faith or fear rule my actions today?

Today I gave of my time ___, talent ___, treasure ___, and touch ___.

Who did I help today?

What am I grateful for today?

Who needs my prayers today?

God, forgive me where I have been resentful, selfish, dishonest, or afraid today. Help me not to keep anything to myself, but to discuss it openly with another person. Show me where I owe an apology and help me make it, and help me to be kind and loving to all people. Use me in the mainstream of life, and remove worry, remorse, and morbid reflection that I may be of service to others. Amen.

When I retire at night…   /   /

Chronology of today's events:

Was I resentful?
1. *Who/what*
2. *Cause*
3. *Affects*
4. *My part*

Was I selfish?

Was I dishonest?

Was I afraid?

Do I owe an apology?

What have I wrongly kept secret?

Was I kind and loving toward all?

What could I have done better?

How did faith or fear rule my actions today?

Today I gave of my time ___, talent ___, treasure ___, and touch ___.

Who did I help today?

What am I grateful for today?

Who needs my prayers today?

God, forgive me where I have been resentful, selfish, dishonest, or afraid today. Help me not to keep anything to myself, but to discuss it openly with another person. Show me where I owe an apology and help me make it, and help me to be kind and loving to all people. Use me in the mainstream of life, and remove worry, remorse, and morbid reflection that I may be of service to others. Amen.

When I retire at night...   /   /

Chronology of today's events:

Was I resentful?
    1. Who/what   3.   Affects

    2. Cause   4.   My part

Was I selfish?

Was I dishonest?

Was I afraid?

Do I owe an apology?

What have I wrongly kept secret?

Was I kind and loving toward all?

What could I have done better?

How did faith or fear rule my actions today?

Today I gave of my time ___, talent ___, treasure ___, and touch ___.

Who did I help today?

What am I grateful for today?

Who needs my prayers today?

God, forgive me where I have been resentful, selfish, dishonest, or afraid today. Help me not to keep anything to myself, but to discuss it openly with another person. Show me where I owe an apology and help me make it, and help me to be kind and loving to all people. Use me in the mainstream of life, and remove worry, remorse, and morbid reflection that I may be of service to others. Amen.

When I retire at night...   /   /

Chronology of today's events:

Was I resentful?
    1. *Who/what*   3. *Affects*

    2. *Cause*   4. *My part*

Was I selfish?

Was I dishonest?

Was I afraid?

Do I owe an apology?

What have I wrongly kept secret?

Was I kind and loving toward all?

What could I have done better?

How did faith or fear rule my actions today?

Today I gave of my time ___, talent ___, treasure ___, and touch ___.

Who did I help today?

What am I grateful for today?

Who needs my prayers today?

God, forgive me where I have been resentful, selfish, dishonest, or afraid today. Help me not to keep anything to myself, but to discuss it openly with another person. Show me where I owe an apology and help me make it, and help me to be kind and loving to all people. Use me in the mainstream of life, and remove worry, remorse, and morbid reflection that I may be of service to others. Amen.

When I retire at night...   /   /

Chronology of today's events:

Was I resentful?
    1. *Who/what*   3. *Affects*

    2. *Cause*   4. *My part*

Was I selfish?

Was I dishonest?

Was I afraid?

Do I owe an apology?

What have I wrongly kept secret?

Was I kind and loving toward all?

What could I have done better?

How did faith or fear rule my actions today?

Today I gave of my time ___, talent ___, treasure ___, and touch ___.

Who did I help today?

What am I grateful for today?

Who needs my prayers today?

God, forgive me where I have been resentful, selfish, dishonest, or afraid today. Help me not to keep anything to myself, but to discuss it openly with another person. Show me where I owe an apology and help me make it, and help me to be kind and loving to all people. Use me in the mainstream of life, and remove worry, remorse, and morbid reflection that I may be of service to others. Amen.

When I retire at night...   /   /

Chronology of today's events:

Was I resentful?
    1. *Who/what*   3. *Affects*

    2. *Cause*   4. *My part*

Was I selfish?

Was I dishonest?

Was I afraid?

Do I owe an apology?

What have I wrongly kept secret?

Was I kind and loving toward all?

What could I have done better?

How did faith or fear rule my actions today?

Today I gave of my time ___, talent ___, treasure ___, and touch ___.

Who did I help today?

What am I grateful for today?

Who needs my prayers today?

God, forgive me where I have been resentful, selfish, dishonest, or afraid today. Help me not to keep anything to myself, but to discuss it openly with another person. Show me where I owe an apology and help me make it, and help me to be kind and loving to all people. Use me in the mainstream of life, and remove worry, remorse, and morbid reflection that I may be of service to others. Amen.

When I retire at night...   /   /

Chronology of today's events:

Was I resentful?
    1. *Who / what*   3. *Affects*

    2. *Cause*   4. *My part*

Was I selfish?

Was I dishonest?

Was I afraid?

Do I owe an apology?

What have I wrongly kept secret?

Was I kind and loving toward all?

What could I have done better?

How did faith or fear rule my actions today?

Today I gave of my time ___, talent ___, treasure ___, and touch ___.

Who did I help today?

What am I grateful for today?

Who needs my prayers today?

God, forgive me where I have been resentful, selfish, dishonest, or afraid today. Help me not to keep anything to myself, but to discuss it openly with another person. Show me where I owe an apology and help me make it, and help me to be kind and loving to all people. Use me in the mainstream of life, and remove worry, remorse, and morbid reflection that I may be of service to others. Amen.

When I retire at night...   /   /

Chronology of today's events:

_____

_____

Was I resentful?
    1. *Who/what*   3. *Affects*

    2. *Cause*   4. *My part*

Was I selfish?

Was I dishonest?

Was I afraid?

Do I owe an apology?

What have I wrongly kept secret?

Was I kind and loving toward all?

What could I have done better?

How did faith or fear rule my actions today?

Today I gave of my time ___, talent ___, treasure ___, and touch ___.

Who did I help today?

What am I grateful for today?

Who needs my prayers today?

God, forgive me where I have been resentful, selfish, dishonest, or afraid today. Help me not to keep anything to myself, but to discuss it openly with another person. Show me where I owe an apology and help me make it, and help me to be kind and loving to all people. Use me in the mainstream of life, and remove worry, remorse, and morbid reflection that I may be of service to others. Amen.

When I retire at night...   /   /

Chronology of today's events:

Was I resentful?
    1. Who/what   3. Affects

    2. Cause   4. My part

Was I selfish?

Was I dishonest?

Was I afraid?

Do I owe an apology?

What have I wrongly kept secret?

Was I kind and loving toward all?

What could I have done better?

How did faith or fear rule my actions today?

Today I gave of my time ___, talent ___, treasure ___, and touch ___.

Who did I help today?

What am I grateful for today?

Who needs my prayers today?

God, forgive me where I have been resentful, selfish, dishonest, or afraid today. Help me not to keep anything to myself, but to discuss it openly with another person. Show me where I owe an apology and help me make it, and help me to be kind and loving to all people. Use me in the mainstream of life, and remove worry, remorse, and morbid reflection that I may be of service to others. Amen.

When I retire at night...   /   /

Chronology of today's events:

Was I resentful?
    1. *Who/what*   3. *Affects*

    2. *Cause*   4. *My part*

Was I selfish?

Was I dishonest?

Was I afraid?

Do I owe an apology?

What have I wrongly kept secret?

Was I kind and loving toward all?

What could I have done better?

How did faith or fear rule my actions today?

Today I gave of my time ___, talent ___, treasure ___, and touch ___.

Who did I help today?

What am I grateful for today?

Who needs my prayers today?

God, forgive me where I have been resentful, selfish, dishonest, or afraid today. Help me not to keep anything to myself, but to discuss it openly with another person. Show me where I owe an apology and help me make it, and help me to be kind and loving to all people. Use me in the mainstream of life, and remove worry, remorse, and morbid reflection that I may be of service to others. Amen.

When I retire at night...   /   /

Chronology of today's events:

Was I resentful?
   1. *Who/what*   3. *Affects*
   2. *Cause*   4. *My part*

Was I selfish?

Was I dishonest?

Was I afraid?

Do I owe an apology?

What have I wrongly kept secret?

Was I kind and loving toward all?

What could I have done better?

How did faith or fear rule my actions today?

Today I gave of my time ___, talent ___, treasure ___, and touch ___.

Who did I help today?

What am I grateful for today?

Who needs my prayers today?

God, forgive me where I have been resentful, selfish, dishonest, or afraid today. Help me not to keep anything to myself, but to discuss it openly with another person. Show me where I owe an apology and help me make it, and help me to be kind and loving to all people. Use me in the mainstream of life, and remove worry, remorse, and morbid reflection that I may be of service to others. Amen.

When I retire at night...   /   /

Chronology of today's events:

Was I resentful?
    1. *Who/what*   3. *Affects*

    2. *Cause*   4. *My part*

Was I selfish?

Was I dishonest?

Was I afraid?

Do I owe an apology?

What have I wrongly kept secret?

Was I kind and loving toward all?

What could I have done better?

How did faith or fear rule my actions today?

Today I gave of my time ___, talent ___, treasure ___, and touch ___.

Who did I help today?

What am I grateful for today?

Who needs my prayers today?

God, forgive me where I have been resentful, selfish, dishonest, or afraid today. Help me not to keep anything to myself, but to discuss it openly with another person. Show me where I owe an apology and help me make it, and help me to be kind and loving to all people. Use me in the mainstream of life, and remove worry, remorse, and morbid reflection that I may be of service to others. Amen.

When I retire at night...   /   /

Chronology of today's events:

Was I resentful?
    1. Who/what   3.   Affects

    2. Cause   4.   My part

Was I selfish?

Was I dishonest?

Was I afraid?

Do I owe an apology?

What have I wrongly kept secret?

Was I kind and loving toward all?

What could I have done better?

How did faith or fear rule my actions today?

Today I gave of my time ___, talent ___, treasure ___, and touch ___.

Who did I help today?

What am I grateful for today?

Who needs my prayers today?

God, forgive me where I have been resentful, selfish, dishonest, or afraid today. Help me not to keep anything to myself, but to discuss it openly with another person. Show me where I owe an apology and help me make it, and help me to be kind and loving to all people. Use me in the mainstream of life, and remove worry, remorse, and morbid reflection that I may be of service to others. Amen.

When I retire at night...   /   /

Chronology of today's events:

Was I resentful?
    1. *Who/what*   3. *Affects*

    2. *Cause*   4. *My part*

Was I selfish?

Was I dishonest?

Was I afraid?

Do I owe an apology?

What have I wrongly kept secret?

Was I kind and loving toward all?

What could I have done better?

How did faith or fear rule my actions today?

Today I gave of my time ___, talent ___, treasure ___, and touch ___.

Who did I help today?

What am I grateful for today?

Who needs my prayers today?

God, forgive me where I have been resentful, selfish, dishonest, or afraid today. Help me not to keep anything to myself, but to discuss it openly with another person. Show me where I owe an apology and help me make it, and help me to be kind and loving to all people. Use me in the mainstream of life, and remove worry, remorse, and morbid reflection that I may be of service to others. Amen.

When I retire at night...   /   /

Chronology of today's events:

Was I resentful?
    1. Who/what   3. Affects

    2. Cause   4. My part

Was I selfish?

Was I dishonest?

Was I afraid?

Do I owe an apology?

What have I wrongly kept secret?

Was I kind and loving toward all?

What could I have done better?

How did faith or fear rule my actions today?

Today I gave of my time ___, talent ___, treasure ___, and touch ___.

Who did I help today?

What am I grateful for today?

Who needs my prayers today?

God, forgive me where I have been resentful, selfish, dishonest, or afraid today. Help me not to keep anything to myself, but to discuss it openly with another person. Show me where I owe an apology and help me make it, and help me to be kind and loving to all people. Use me in the mainstream of life, and remove worry, remorse, and morbid reflection that I may be of service to others. Amen.

When I retire at night...   /   /

Chronology of today's events:

_____
_____
_____

Was I resentful?
    1. *Who/what*   3. *Affects*

    2. *Cause*   4. *My part*

Was I selfish?

Was I dishonest?

Was I afraid?

Do I owe an apology?

What have I wrongly kept secret?

Was I kind and loving toward all?

What could I have done better?

How did faith or fear rule my actions today?

Today I gave of my time ___, talent ___, treasure ___, and touch ___.

Who did I help today?

What am I grateful for today?

Who needs my prayers today?

God, forgive me where I have been resentful, selfish, dishonest, or afraid today. Help me not to keep anything to myself, but to discuss it openly with another person. Show me where I owe an apology and help me make it, and help me to be kind and loving to all people. Use me in the mainstream of life, and remove worry, remorse, and morbid reflection that I may be of service to others. Amen.

When I retire at night...   /   /

Chronology of today's events:

Was I resentful?
    1. *Who/what*　　　　　　　　3. *Affects*

    2. *Cause*　　　　　　　　　　4. *My part*

Was I selfish?

Was I dishonest?

Was I afraid?

Do I owe an apology?

What have I wrongly kept secret?

Was I kind and loving toward all?

What could I have done better?

How did faith or fear rule my actions today?

Today I gave of my time ___, talent ___, treasure ___, and touch ___.

Who did I help today?

What am I grateful for today?

Who needs my prayers today?

God, forgive me where I have been resentful, selfish, dishonest, or afraid today. Help me not to keep anything to myself, but to discuss it openly with another person. Show me where I owe an apology and help me make it, and help me to be kind and loving to all people. Use me in the mainstream of life, and remove worry, remorse, and morbid reflection that I may be of service to others. Amen.

When I retire at night...   /   /

Chronology of today's events:

Was I resentful?
    1. *Who/what*   3. *Affects*

    2. *Cause*   4. *My part*

Was I selfish?

Was I dishonest?

Was I afraid?

Do I owe an apology?

What have I wrongly kept secret?

Was I kind and loving toward all?

What could I have done better?

How did faith or fear rule my actions today?

Today I gave of my time ___, talent ___, treasure ___, and touch ___.

Who did I help today?

What am I grateful for today?

Who needs my prayers today?

God, forgive me where I have been resentful, selfish, dishonest, or afraid today. Help me not to keep anything to myself, but to discuss it openly with another person. Show me where I owe an apology and help me make it, and help me to be kind and loving to all people. Use me in the mainstream of life, and remove worry, remorse, and morbid reflection that I may be of service to others. Amen.

When I retire at night…   /   /

Chronology of today's events:

Was I resentful?
    1. *Who/what*   3.   *Affects*

    2. *Cause*   4.   *My part*

Was I selfish?

Was I dishonest?

Was I afraid?

Do I owe an apology?

What have I wrongly kept secret?

Was I kind and loving toward all?

What could I have done better?

How did faith or fear rule my actions today?

Today I gave of my time ___, talent ___, treasure ___, and touch ___.

Who did I help today?

What am I grateful for today?

Who needs my prayers today?

God, forgive me where I have been resentful, selfish, dishonest, or afraid today. Help me not to keep anything to myself, but to discuss it openly with another person. Show me where I owe an apology and help me make it, and help me to be kind and loving to all people. Use me in the mainstream of life, and remove worry, remorse, and morbid reflection that I may be of service to others. Amen.

When I retire at night...   /   /

Chronology of today's events:

Was I resentful?
    1. *Who/what*   3. *Affects*

    2. *Cause*   4. *My part*

Was I selfish?

Was I dishonest?

Was I afraid?

Do I owe an apology?

What have I wrongly kept secret?

Was I kind and loving toward all?

What could I have done better?

How did faith or fear rule my actions today?

Today I gave of my time ___, talent ___, treasure ___, and touch ___.

Who did I help today?

What am I grateful for today?

Who needs my prayers today?

God, forgive me where I have been resentful, selfish, dishonest, or afraid today. Help me not to keep anything to myself, but to discuss it openly with another person. Show me where I owe an apology and help me make it, and help me to be kind and loving to all people. Use me in the mainstream of life, and remove worry, remorse, and morbid reflection that I may be of service to others. Amen.

When I retire at night...   /   /

Chronology of today's events:

Was I resentful?
    1. Who/what   3.   Affects

    2. Cause   4.   My part

Was I selfish?

Was I dishonest?

Was I afraid?

Do I owe an apology?

What have I wrongly kept secret?

Was I kind and loving toward all?

What could I have done better?

How did faith or fear rule my actions today?

Today I gave of my time ___, talent ___, treasure ___, and touch ___.

Who did I help today?

What am I grateful for today?

Who needs my prayers today?

God, forgive me where I have been resentful, selfish, dishonest, or afraid today. Help me not to keep anything to myself, but to discuss it openly with another person. Show me where I owe an apology and help me make it, and help me to be kind and loving to all people. Use me in the mainstream of life, and remove worry, remorse, and morbid reflection that I may be of service to others. Amen.

When I retire at night...   /   /

Chronology of today's events:
_____
_____

Was I resentful?
    1. Who/what   3. Affects

    2. Cause   4. My part

Was I selfish?

Was I dishonest?

Was I afraid?

Do I owe an apology?

What have I wrongly kept secret?

Was I kind and loving toward all?

What could I have done better?

How did faith or fear rule my actions today?

Today I gave of my time ___, talent ___, treasure ___, and touch ___.

Who did I help today?

What am I grateful for today?

Who needs my prayers today?

God, forgive me where I have been resentful, selfish, dishonest, or afraid today. Help me not to keep anything to myself, but to discuss it openly with another person. Show me where I owe an apology and help me make it, and help me to be kind and loving to all people. Use me in the mainstream of life, and remove worry, remorse, and morbid reflection that I may be of service to others. Amen.

When I retire at night...   /   /

Chronology of today's events:

Was I resentful?
    1. *Who/what*   3. *Affects*

    2. *Cause*   4. *My part*

Was I selfish?

Was I dishonest?

Was I afraid?

Do I owe an apology?

What have I wrongly kept secret?

Was I kind and loving toward all?

What could I have done better?

How did faith or fear rule my actions today?

Today I gave of my time ____, talent ____, treasure ____, and touch ____.

Who did I help today?

What am I grateful for today?

Who needs my prayers today?

God, forgive me where I have been resentful, selfish, dishonest, or afraid today. Help me not to keep anything to myself, but to discuss it openly with another person. Show me where I owe an apology and help me make it, and help me to be kind and loving to all people. Use me in the mainstream of life, and remove worry, remorse, and morbid reflection that I may be of service to others. Amen.

When I retire at night...   /   /

Chronology of today's events:

Was I resentful?
    1. *Who/what*   3. *Affects*

    2. *Cause*   4. *My part*

Was I selfish?

Was I dishonest?

Was I afraid?

Do I owe an apology?

What have I wrongly kept secret?

Was I kind and loving toward all?

What could I have done better?

How did faith or fear rule my actions today?

Today I gave of my time ___, talent ___, treasure ___, and touch ___.

Who did I help today?

What am I grateful for today?

Who needs my prayers today?

God, forgive me where I have been resentful, selfish, dishonest, or afraid today. Help me not to keep anything to myself, but to discuss it openly with another person. Show me where I owe an apology and help me make it, and help me to be kind and loving to all people. Use me in the mainstream of life, and remove worry, remorse, and morbid reflection that I may be of service to others. Amen.

When I retire at night…   /   /

Chronology of today's events:

Was I resentful?
    1. *Who/what*   3.   *Affects*

    2. *Cause*   4.   *My part*

Was I selfish?

Was I dishonest?

Was I afraid?

Do I owe an apology?

What have I wrongly kept secret?

Was I kind and loving toward all?

What could I have done better?

How did faith or fear rule my actions today?

Today I gave of my time ___, talent ___, treasure ___, and touch ___.

Who did I help today?

What am I grateful for today?

Who needs my prayers today?

God, forgive me where I have been resentful, selfish, dishonest, or afraid today. Help me not to keep anything to myself, but to discuss it openly with another person. Show me where I owe an apology and help me make it, and help me to be kind and loving to all people. Use me in the mainstream of life, and remove worry, remorse, and morbid reflection that I may be of service to others. Amen.

When I retire at night...   /   /

Chronology of today's events:

Was I resentful?
    1. *Who/what*   3. *Affects*

    2. *Cause*   4. *My part*

Was I selfish?

Was I dishonest?

Was I afraid?

Do I owe an apology?

What have I wrongly kept secret?

Was I kind and loving toward all?

What could I have done better?

How did faith or fear rule my actions today?

Today I gave of my time ___, talent ___, treasure ___, and touch ___.

Who did I help today?

What am I grateful for today?

Who needs my prayers today?

God, forgive me where I have been resentful, selfish, dishonest, or afraid today. Help me not to keep anything to myself, but to discuss it openly with another person. Show me where I owe an apology and help me make it, and help me to be kind and loving to all people. Use me in the mainstream of life, and remove worry, remorse, and morbid reflection that I may be of service to others. Amen.

When I retire at night...   /   /

Chronology of today's events:

Was I resentful?
    1. *Who/what*   3. *Affects*

    2. *Cause*   4. *My part*

Was I selfish?

Was I dishonest?

Was I afraid?

Do I owe an apology?

What have I wrongly kept secret?

Was I kind and loving toward all?

What could I have done better?

How did faith or fear rule my actions today?

Today I gave of my time ___, talent ___, treasure ___, and touch ___.

Who did I help today?

What am I grateful for today?

Who needs my prayers today?

God, forgive me where I have been resentful, selfish, dishonest, or afraid today. Help me not to keep anything to myself, but to discuss it openly with another person. Show me where I owe an apology and help me make it, and help me to be kind and loving to all people. Use me in the mainstream of life, and remove worry, remorse, and morbid reflection that I may be of service to others. Amen.

When I retire at night...   /   /

Chronology of today's events:

Was I resentful?
    1. *Who/what*   3. *Affects*

    2. *Cause*   4. *My part*

Was I selfish?

Was I dishonest?

Was I afraid?

Do I owe an apology?

What have I wrongly kept secret?

Was I kind and loving toward all?

What could I have done better?

How did faith or fear rule my actions today?

Today I gave of my time ___, talent ___, treasure ___, and touch ___.

Who did I help today?

What am I grateful for today?

Who needs my prayers today?

God, forgive me where I have been resentful, selfish, dishonest, or afraid today. Help me not to keep anything to myself, but to discuss it openly with another person. Show me where I owe an apology and help me make it, and help me to be kind and loving to all people. Use me in the mainstream of life, and remove worry, remorse, and morbid reflection that I may be of service to others. Amen.

When I retire at night…   /   /

Chronology of today's events:

Was I resentful?
    1. *Who/what*   3. *Affects*

    2. *Cause*   4. *My part*

Was I selfish?

Was I dishonest?

Was I afraid?

Do I owe an apology?

What have I wrongly kept secret?

Was I kind and loving toward all?

What could I have done better?

How did faith or fear rule my actions today?

Today I gave of my time ___, talent ___, treasure ___, and touch ___.

Who did I help today?

What am I grateful for today?

Who needs my prayers today?

God, forgive me where I have been resentful, selfish, dishonest, or afraid today. Help me not to keep anything to myself, but to discuss it openly with another person. Show me where I owe an apology and help me make it, and help me to be kind and loving to all people. Use me in the mainstream of life, and remove worry, remorse, and morbid reflection that I may be of service to others. Amen.

When I retire at night...   /   /

Chronology of today's events:

Was I resentful?
    1. *Who/what*   3. *Affects*

    2. *Cause*   4. *My part*

Was I selfish?

Was I dishonest?

Was I afraid?

Do I owe an apology?

What have I wrongly kept secret?

Was I kind and loving toward all?

What could I have done better?

How did faith or fear rule my actions today?

Today I gave of my time ___, talent ___, treasure ___, and touch ___.

Who did I help today?

What am I grateful for today?

Who needs my prayers today?

God, forgive me where I have been resentful, selfish, dishonest, or afraid today. Help me not to keep anything to myself, but to discuss it openly with another person. Show me where I owe an apology and help me make it, and help me to be kind and loving to all people. Use me in the mainstream of life, and remove worry, remorse, and morbid reflection that I may be of service to others. Amen.

When I retire at night...   /   /

Chronology of today's events:

Was I resentful?
    1. *Who/what*　　　　　　　3. *Affects*

    2. *Cause*　　　　　　　　　4. *My part*

Was I selfish?

Was I dishonest?

Was I afraid?

Do I owe an apology?

What have I wrongly kept secret?

Was I kind and loving toward all?

What could I have done better?

How did faith or fear rule my actions today?

Today I gave of my time ___, talent ___, treasure ___, and touch ___.

Who did I help today?

What am I grateful for today?

Who needs my prayers today?

God, forgive me where I have been resentful, selfish, dishonest, or afraid today. Help me not to keep anything to myself, but to discuss it openly with another person. Show me where I owe an apology and help me make it, and help me to be kind and loving to all people. Use me in the mainstream of life, and remove worry, remorse, and morbid reflection that I may be of service to others. Amen.

When I retire at night...   /   /

Chronology of today's events:

Was I resentful?
    1. *Who/what*   3. *Affects*

    2. *Cause*   4. *My part*

Was I selfish?

Was I dishonest?

Was I afraid?

Do I owe an apology?

What have I wrongly kept secret?

Was I kind and loving toward all?

What could I have done better?

How did faith or fear rule my actions today?

Today I gave of my time ___, talent ___, treasure ___, and touch ___.

Who did I help today?

What am I grateful for today?

Who needs my prayers today?

God, forgive me where I have been resentful, selfish, dishonest, or afraid today. Help me not to keep anything to myself, but to discuss it openly with another person. Show me where I owe an apology and help me make it, and help me to be kind and loving to all people. Use me in the mainstream of life, and remove worry, remorse, and morbid reflection that I may be of service to others. Amen.

When I retire at night…   /   /

Chronology of today's events:

Was I resentful?
    1. Who/what   3. Affects

    2. Cause   4. My part

Was I selfish?

Was I dishonest?

Was I afraid?

Do I owe an apology?

What have I wrongly kept secret?

Was I kind and loving toward all?

What could I have done better?

How did faith or fear rule my actions today?

Today I gave of my time ___, talent ___, treasure ___, and touch ___.

Who did I help today?

What am I grateful for today?

Who needs my prayers today?

God, forgive me where I have been resentful, selfish, dishonest, or afraid today. Help me not to keep anything to myself, but to discuss it openly with another person. Show me where I owe an apology and help me make it, and help me to be kind and loving to all people. Use me in the mainstream of life, and remove worry, remorse, and morbid reflection that I may be of service to others. Amen.

When I retire at night...   /   /

Chronology of today's events:

Was I resentful?
    1. Who/what　　　　　　　　3. Affects

    2. Cause　　　　　　　　　　4. My part

Was I selfish?

Was I dishonest?

Was I afraid?

Do I owe an apology?

What have I wrongly kept secret?

Was I kind and loving toward all?

What could I have done better?

How did faith or fear rule my actions today?

Today I gave of my time ___, talent ___, treasure ___, and touch ___.

Who did I help today?

What am I grateful for today?

Who needs my prayers today?

God, forgive me where I have been resentful, selfish, dishonest, or afraid today. Help me not to keep anything to myself, but to discuss it openly with another person. Show me where I owe an apology and help me make it, and help me to be kind and loving to all people. Use me in the mainstream of life, and remove worry, remorse, and morbid reflection that I may be of service to others. Amen.

When I retire at night...   /   /

Chronology of today's events:

Was I resentful?
    1. *Who/what*   3. *Affects*

    2. *Cause*   4. *My part*

Was I selfish?

Was I dishonest?

Was I afraid?

Do I owe an apology?

What have I wrongly kept secret?

Was I kind and loving toward all?

What could I have done better?

How did faith or fear rule my actions today?

Today I gave of my time ___, talent ___, treasure ___, and touch ___.

Who did I help today?

What am I grateful for today?

Who needs my prayers today?

God, forgive me where I have been resentful, selfish, dishonest, or afraid today. Help me not to keep anything to myself, but to discuss it openly with another person. Show me where I owe an apology and help me make it, and help me to be kind and loving to all people. Use me in the mainstream of life, and remove worry, remorse, and morbid reflection that I may be of service to others. Amen.

When I retire at night...   /   /

Chronology of today's events:

Was I resentful?
    1. *Who/what*
    2. *Cause*
    3. *Affects*
    4. *My part*

Was I selfish?

Was I dishonest?

Was I afraid?

Do I owe an apology?

What have I wrongly kept secret?

Was I kind and loving toward all?

What could I have done better?

How did faith or fear rule my actions today?

Today I gave of my time ___, talent ___, treasure ___, and touch ___.

Who did I help today?

What am I grateful for today?

Who needs my prayers today?

God, forgive me where I have been resentful, selfish, dishonest, or afraid today. Help me not to keep anything to myself, but to discuss it openly with another person. Show me where I owe an apology and help me make it, and help me to be kind and loving to all people. Use me in the mainstream of life, and remove worry, remorse, and morbid reflection that I may be of service to others. Amen.

When I retire at night...   /   /

Chronology of today's events:

Was I resentful?
    1. *Who/what*   3.   *Affects*

    2. *Cause*   4.   *My part*

Was I selfish?

Was I dishonest?

Was I afraid?

Do I owe an apology?

What have I wrongly kept secret?

Was I kind and loving toward all?

What could I have done better?

How did faith or fear rule my actions today?

Today I gave of my time ___, talent ___, treasure ___, and touch ___.

Who did I help today?

What am I grateful for today?

Who needs my prayers today?

God, forgive me where I have been resentful, selfish, dishonest, or afraid today. Help me not to keep anything to myself, but to discuss it openly with another person. Show me where I owe an apology and help me make it, and help me to be kind and loving to all people. Use me in the mainstream of life, and remove worry, remorse, and morbid reflection that I may be of service to others. Amen.

When I retire at night...   /   /

Chronology of today's events:

Was I resentful?
    1. *Who/what*   3. *Affects*

    2. *Cause*   4. *My part*

Was I selfish?

Was I dishonest?

Was I afraid?

Do I owe an apology?

What have I wrongly kept secret?

Was I kind and loving toward all?

What could I have done better?

How did faith or fear rule my actions today?

Today I gave of my time ___, talent ___, treasure ___, and touch ___.

Who did I help today?

What am I grateful for today?

Who needs my prayers today?

God, forgive me where I have been resentful, selfish, dishonest, or afraid today. Help me not to keep anything to myself, but to discuss it openly with another person. Show me where I owe an apology and help me make it, and help me to be kind and loving to all people. Use me in the mainstream of life, and remove worry, remorse, and morbid reflection that I may be of service to others. Amen.

When I retire at night...   /   /

Chronology of today's events:

Was I resentful?
    1. Who/what   *3. Affects*

    2. Cause   *4. My part*

Was I selfish?

Was I dishonest?

Was I afraid?

Do I owe an apology?

What have I wrongly kept secret?

Was I kind and loving toward all?

What could I have done better?

How did faith or fear rule my actions today?

Today I gave of my time ___, talent ___, treasure ___, and touch ___ .

Who did I help today?

What am I grateful for today?

Who needs my prayers today?

God, forgive me where I have been resentful, selfish, dishonest, or afraid today. Help me not to keep anything to myself, but to discuss it openly with another person. Show me where I owe an apology and help me make it, and help me to be kind and loving to all people. Use me in the mainstream of life, and remove worry, remorse, and morbid reflection that I may be of service to others. Amen.

When I retire at night...   /   /

Chronology of today's events:

Was I resentful?
    1. Who/what   3. Affects

    2. Cause   4. My part

Was I selfish?

Was I dishonest?

Was I afraid?

Do I owe an apology?

What have I wrongly kept secret?

Was I kind and loving toward all?

What could I have done better?

How did faith or fear rule my actions today?

Today I gave of my time ___, talent ___, treasure ___, and touch ___.

Who did I help today?

What am I grateful for today?

Who needs my prayers today?

God, forgive me where I have been resentful, selfish, dishonest, or afraid today. Help me not to keep anything to myself, but to discuss it openly with another person. Show me where I owe an apology and help me make it, and help me to be kind and loving to all people. Use me in the mainstream of life, and remove worry, remorse, and morbid reflection that I may be of service to others. Amen.

When I retire at night...   /   /

Chronology of today's events:

Was I resentful?
    1. *Who/what*   3. *Affects*

    2. *Cause*   4. *My part*

Was I selfish?

Was I dishonest?

Was I afraid?

Do I owe an apology?

What have I wrongly kept secret?

Was I kind and loving toward all?

What could I have done better?

How did faith or fear rule my actions today?

Today I gave of my time ___, talent ___, treasure ___, and touch ___.

Who did I help today?

What am I grateful for today?

Who needs my prayers today?

God, forgive me where I have been resentful, selfish, dishonest, or afraid today. Help me not to keep anything to myself, but to discuss it openly with another person. Show me where I owe an apology and help me make it, and help me to be kind and loving to all people. Use me in the mainstream of life, and remove worry, remorse, and morbid reflection that I may be of service to others. Amen.

When I retire at night…   /   /

Chronology of today's events:

Was I resentful?
    1. *Who/what*   3. *Affects*

    2. *Cause*   4. *My part*

Was I selfish?

Was I dishonest?

Was I afraid?

Do I owe an apology?

What have I wrongly kept secret?

Was I kind and loving toward all?

What could I have done better?

How did faith or fear rule my actions today?

Today I gave of my time ___, talent ___, treasure ___, and touch ___.

Who did I help today?

What am I grateful for today?

Who needs my prayers today?

God, forgive me where I have been resentful, selfish, dishonest, or afraid today. Help me not to keep anything to myself, but to discuss it openly with another person. Show me where I owe an apology and help me make it, and help me to be kind and loving to all people. Use me in the mainstream of life, and remove worry, remorse, and morbid reflection that I may be of service to others. Amen.

When I retire at night...   /   /

Chronology of today's events:

Was I resentful?
    1. Who/what   3. Affects

    2. Cause   4. My part

Was I selfish?

Was I dishonest?

Was I afraid?

Do I owe an apology?

What have I wrongly kept secret?

Was I kind and loving toward all?

What could I have done better?

How did faith or fear rule my actions today?

Today I gave of my time ___, talent ___, treasure ___, and touch ___.

Who did I help today?

What am I grateful for today?

Who needs my prayers today?

God, forgive me where I have been resentful, selfish, dishonest, or afraid today. Help me not to keep anything to myself, but to discuss it openly with another person. Show me where I owe an apology and help me make it, and help me to be kind and loving to all people. Use me in the mainstream of life, and remove worry, remorse, and morbid reflection that I may be of service to others. Amen.

When I retire at night…   /   /

Chronology of today's events:

Was I resentful?
    1. Who/what   *3. Affects*

    2. Cause   *4. My part*

Was I selfish?

Was I dishonest?

Was I afraid?

Do I owe an apology?

What have I wrongly kept secret?

Was I kind and loving toward all?

What could I have done better?

How did faith or fear rule my actions today?

Today I gave of my time ___, talent ___, treasure ___, and touch ___.

Who did I help today?

What am I grateful for today?

Who needs my prayers today?

God, forgive me where I have been resentful, selfish, dishonest, or afraid today. Help me not to keep anything to myself, but to discuss it openly with another person. Show me where I owe an apology and help me make it, and help me to be kind and loving to all people. Use me in the mainstream of life, and remove worry, remorse, and morbid reflection that I may be of service to others. Amen.

When I retire at night…   /   /

Chronology of today's events:

Was I resentful?
    1. Who/what   3. Affects

    2. Cause   4. My part

Was I selfish?

Was I dishonest?

Was I afraid?

Do I owe an apology?

What have I wrongly kept secret?

Was I kind and loving toward all?

What could I have done better?

How did faith or fear rule my actions today?

Today I gave of my time ___, talent ___, treasure ___, and touch ___.

Who did I help today?

What am I grateful for today?

Who needs my prayers today?

God, forgive me where I have been resentful, selfish, dishonest, or afraid today. Help me not to keep anything to myself, but to discuss it openly with another person. Show me where I owe an apology and help me make it, and help me to be kind and loving to all people. Use me in the mainstream of life, and remove worry, remorse, and morbid reflection that I may be of service to others. Amen.

When I retire at night...   /   /

Chronology of today's events:

Was I resentful?
  1. *Who/what*   3. *Affects*
  2. *Cause*   4. *My part*

Was I selfish?

Was I dishonest?

Was I afraid?

Do I owe an apology?

What have I wrongly kept secret?

Was I kind and loving toward all?

What could I have done better?

How did faith or fear rule my actions today?

Today I gave of my time ___, talent ___, treasure ___, and touch ___.

Who did I help today?

What am I grateful for today?

Who needs my prayers today?

God, forgive me where I have been resentful, selfish, dishonest, or afraid today. Help me not to keep anything to myself, but to discuss it openly with another person. Show me where I owe an apology and help me make it, and help me to be kind and loving to all people. Use me in the mainstream of life, and remove worry, remorse, and morbid reflection that I may be of service to others. Amen.

When I retire at night...   /   /

Chronology of today's events:

Was I resentful?
    1. *Who/what*   3.   *Affects*

    2. *Cause*   4.   *My part*

Was I selfish?

Was I dishonest?

Was I afraid?

Do I owe an apology?

What have I wrongly kept secret?

Was I kind and loving toward all?

What could I have done better?

How did faith or fear rule my actions today?

Today I gave of my time ___, talent ___, treasure ___, and touch ___.

Who did I help today?

What am I grateful for today?

Who needs my prayers today?

God, forgive me where I have been resentful, selfish, dishonest, or afraid today. Help me not to keep anything to myself, but to discuss it openly with another person. Show me where I owe an apology and help me make it, and help me to be kind and loving to all people. Use me in the mainstream of life, and remove worry, remorse, and morbid reflection that I may be of service to others. Amen.

When I retire at night...   /   /

Chronology of today's events:

Was I resentful?
    1. *Who/what*   3. *Affects*

    2. *Cause*   4. *My part*

Was I selfish?

Was I dishonest?

Was I afraid?

Do I owe an apology?

What have I wrongly kept secret?

Was I kind and loving toward all?

What could I have done better?

How did faith or fear rule my actions today?

Today I gave of my time ___, talent ___, treasure ___, and touch ___.

Who did I help today?

What am I grateful for today?

Who needs my prayers today?

God, forgive me where I have been resentful, selfish, dishonest, or afraid today. Help me not to keep anything to myself, but to discuss it openly with another person. Show me where I owe an apology and help me make it, and help me to be kind and loving to all people. Use me in the mainstream of life, and remove worry, remorse, and morbid reflection that I may be of service to others. Amen.

When I retire at night...   /   /

Chronology of today's events:

Was I resentful?
    1. *Who/what*   3.   *Affects*

    2. *Cause*   4.   *My part*

Was I selfish?

Was I dishonest?

Was I afraid?

Do I owe an apology?

What have I wrongly kept secret?

Was I kind and loving toward all?

What could I have done better?

How did faith or fear rule my actions today?

Today I gave of my time ___, talent ___, treasure ___, and touch ___.

Who did I help today?

What am I grateful for today?

Who needs my prayers today?

God, forgive me where I have been resentful, selfish, dishonest, or afraid today. Help me not to keep anything to myself, but to discuss it openly with another person. Show me where I owe an apology and help me make it, and help me to be kind and loving to all people. Use me in the mainstream of life, and remove worry, remorse, and morbid reflection that I may be of service to others. Amen.

When I retire at night...   /   /

Chronology of today's events:

Was I resentful?
    1. *Who/what*　　　　　　　3. *Affects*

    2. *Cause*　　　　　　　　　4. *My part*

Was I selfish?

Was I dishonest?

Was I afraid?

Do I owe an apology?

What have I wrongly kept secret?

Was I kind and loving toward all?

What could I have done better?

How did faith or fear rule my actions today?

Today I gave of my time ___, talent ___, treasure ___, and touch ___.

Who did I help today?

What am I grateful for today?

Who needs my prayers today?

God, forgive me where I have been resentful, selfish, dishonest, or afraid today. Help me not to keep anything to myself, but to discuss it openly with another person. Show me where I owe an apology and help me make it, and help me to be kind and loving to all people. Use me in the mainstream of life, and remove worry, remorse, and morbid reflection that I may be of service to others. Amen.

When I retire at night...   /   /

Chronology of today's events:

Was I resentful?
    1. Who/what   3. Affects

    2. Cause   4. My part

Was I selfish?

Was I dishonest?

Was I afraid?

Do I owe an apology?

What have I wrongly kept secret?

Was I kind and loving toward all?

What could I have done better?

How did faith or fear rule my actions today?

Today I gave of my time ___, talent ___, treasure ___, and touch ___.

Who did I help today?

What am I grateful for today?

Who needs my prayers today?

God, forgive me where I have been resentful, selfish, dishonest, or afraid today. Help me not to keep anything to myself, but to discuss it openly with another person. Show me where I owe an apology and help me make it, and help me to be kind and loving to all people. Use me in the mainstream of life, and remove worry, remorse, and morbid reflection that I may be of service to others. Amen.

When I retire at night...   /   /

Chronology of today's events:

___

Was I resentful?

    1. *Who / what*   3. *Affects*

    2. *Cause*   4. *My part*

Was I selfish?

Was I dishonest?

Was I afraid?

Do I owe an apology?

What have I wrongly kept secret?

Was I kind and loving toward all?

What could I have done better?

How did faith or fear rule my actions today?

Today I gave of my time ___, talent ___, treasure ___, and touch ___.

Who did I help today?

What am I grateful for today?

Who needs my prayers today?

God, forgive me where I have been resentful, selfish, dishonest, or afraid today. Help me not to keep anything to myself, but to discuss it openly with another person. Show me where I owe an apology and help me make it, and help me to be kind and loving to all people. Use me in the mainstream of life, and remove worry, remorse, and morbid reflection that I may be of service to others. Amen.

When I retire at night...   /   /

Chronology of today's events:

Was I resentful?
    1. Who/what   *3. Affects*

    2. Cause   *4. My part*

Was I selfish?

Was I dishonest?

Was I afraid?

Do I owe an apology?

What have I wrongly kept secret?

Was I kind and loving toward all?

What could I have done better?

How did faith or fear rule my actions today?

Today I gave of my time ___, talent ___, treasure ___, and touch ___.

Who did I help today?

What am I grateful for today?

Who needs my prayers today?

God, forgive me where I have been resentful, selfish, dishonest, or afraid today. Help me not to keep anything to myself, but to discuss it openly with another person. Show me where I owe an apology and help me make it, and help me to be kind and loving to all people. Use me in the mainstream of life, and remove worry, remorse, and morbid reflection that I may be of service to others. Amen.

When I retire at night...   /   /

Chronology of today's events:

Was I resentful?
   1. *Who/what*   3. *Affects*

   2. *Cause*   4. *My part*

Was I selfish?

Was I dishonest?

Was I afraid?

Do I owe an apology?

What have I wrongly kept secret?

Was I kind and loving toward all?

What could I have done better?

How did faith or fear rule my actions today?

Today I gave of my time ___, talent ___, treasure ___, and touch ___.

Who did I help today?

What am I grateful for today?

Who needs my prayers today?

God, forgive me where I have been resentful, selfish, dishonest, or afraid today. Help me not to keep anything to myself, but to discuss it openly with another person. Show me where I owe an apology and help me make it, and help me to be kind and loving to all people. Use me in the mainstream of life, and remove worry, remorse, and morbid reflection that I may be of service to others. Amen.

When I retire at night…   /   /

Chronology of today's events:

Was I resentful?
    1. *Who/what*   3.   *Affects*

    2. *Cause*   4.   *My part*

Was I selfish?

Was I dishonest?

Was I afraid?

Do I owe an apology?

What have I wrongly kept secret?

Was I kind and loving toward all?

What could I have done better?

How did faith or fear rule my actions today?

Today I gave of my time ___, talent ___, treasure ___, and touch ___.

Who did I help today?

What am I grateful for today?

Who needs my prayers today?

God, forgive me where I have been resentful, selfish, dishonest, or afraid today. Help me not to keep anything to myself, but to discuss it openly with another person. Show me where I owe an apology and help me make it, and help me to be kind and loving to all people. Use me in the mainstream of life, and remove worry, remorse, and morbid reflection that I may be of service to others. Amen.

When I retire at night...   /   /

Chronology of today's events:

Was I resentful?
    1. *Who/what*   3. *Affects*

    2. *Cause*   4. *My part*

Was I selfish?

Was I dishonest?

Was I afraid?

Do I owe an apology?

What have I wrongly kept secret?

Was I kind and loving toward all?

What could I have done better?

How did faith or fear rule my actions today?

Today I gave of my time ___, talent ___, treasure ___, and touch ___.

Who did I help today?

What am I grateful for today?

Who needs my prayers today?

God, forgive me where I have been resentful, selfish, dishonest, or afraid today. Help me not to keep anything to myself, but to discuss it openly with another person. Show me where I owe an apology and help me make it, and help me to be kind and loving to all people. Use me in the mainstream of life, and remove worry, remorse, and morbid reflection that I may be of service to others. Amen.

When I retire at night…   /   /

Chronology of today's events:

Was I resentful?
    1. Who/what   3. Affects

    2. Cause   4. My part

Was I selfish?

Was I dishonest?

Was I afraid?

Do I owe an apology?

What have I wrongly kept secret?

Was I kind and loving toward all?

What could I have done better?

How did faith or fear rule my actions today?

Today I gave of my time ___, talent ___, treasure ___, and touch ___.

Who did I help today?

What am I grateful for today?

Who needs my prayers today?

God, forgive me where I have been resentful, selfish, dishonest, or afraid today. Help me not to keep anything to myself, but to discuss it openly with another person. Show me where I owe an apology and help me make it, and help me to be kind and loving to all people. Use me in the mainstream of life, and remove worry, remorse, and morbid reflection that I may be of service to others. Amen.

When I retire at night...   /   /

Chronology of today's events:

Was I resentful?

    1. *Who/what*   3. *Affects*

    2. *Cause*   4. *My part*

Was I selfish?

Was I dishonest?

Was I afraid?

Do I owe an apology?

What have I wrongly kept secret?

Was I kind and loving toward all?

What could I have done better?

How did faith or fear rule my actions today?

Today I gave of my time ___, talent ___, treasure ___, and touch ___.

Who did I help today?

What am I grateful for today?

Who needs my prayers today?

God, forgive me where I have been resentful, selfish, dishonest, or afraid today. Help me not to keep anything to myself, but to discuss it openly with another person. Show me where I owe an apology and help me make it, and help me to be kind and loving to all people. Use me in the mainstream of life, and remove worry, remorse, and morbid reflection that I may be of service to others. Amen.

When I retire at night...   /   /

Chronology of today's events:

Was I resentful?
    1. *Who/what*   3. *Affects*

    2. *Cause*   4. *My part*

Was I selfish?

Was I dishonest?

Was I afraid?

Do I owe an apology?

What have I wrongly kept secret?

Was I kind and loving toward all?

What could I have done better?

How did faith or fear rule my actions today?

Today I gave of my time ___, talent ___, treasure ___, and touch ___.

Who did I help today?

What am I grateful for today?

Who needs my prayers today?

God, forgive me where I have been resentful, selfish, dishonest, or afraid today. Help me not to keep anything to myself, but to discuss it openly with another person. Show me where I owe an apology and help me make it, and help me to be kind and loving to all people. Use me in the mainstream of life, and remove worry, remorse, and morbid reflection that I may be of service to others. Amen.

When I retire at night...   /   /

Chronology of today's events:

Was I resentful?

    1. *Who/what*   3. *Affects*

    2. *Cause*   4. *My part*

Was I selfish?

Was I dishonest?

Was I afraid?

Do I owe an apology?

What have I wrongly kept secret?

Was I kind and loving toward all?

What could I have done better?

How did faith or fear rule my actions today?

Today I gave of my time ___, talent ___, treasure ___, and touch ___.

Who did I help today?

What am I grateful for today?

Who needs my prayers today?

God, forgive me where I have been resentful, selfish, dishonest, or afraid today. Help me not to keep anything to myself, but to discuss it openly with another person. Show me where I owe an apology and help me make it, and help me to be kind and loving to all people. Use me in the mainstream of life, and remove worry, remorse, and morbid reflection that I may be of service to others. Amen.

When I retire at night...   /   /

Chronology of today's events:

Was I resentful?
    1. *Who / what*　　　　　　　3. *Affects*

    2. *Cause*　　　　　　　　　　4. *My part*

Was I selfish?

Was I dishonest?

Was I afraid?

Do I owe an apology?

What have I wrongly kept secret?

Was I kind and loving toward all?

What could I have done better?

How did faith or fear rule my actions today?

Today I gave of my time ___, talent ___, treasure ___, and touch ___.

Who did I help today?

What am I grateful for today?

Who needs my prayers today?

God, forgive me where I have been resentful, selfish, dishonest, or afraid today. Help me not to keep anything to myself, but to discuss it openly with another person. Show me where I owe an apology and help me make it, and help me to be kind and loving to all people. Use me in the mainstream of life, and remove worry, remorse, and morbid reflection that I may be of service to others. Amen.

When I retire at night...   /   /

Chronology of today's events:

Was I resentful?
    1. *Who/what*   3.   *Affects*

    2. *Cause*   4.   *My part*

Was I selfish?

Was I dishonest?

Was I afraid?

Do I owe an apology?

What have I wrongly kept secret?

Was I kind and loving toward all?

What could I have done better?

How did faith or fear rule my actions today?

Today I gave of my time ___, talent ___, treasure ___, and touch ___.

Who did I help today?

What am I grateful for today?

Who needs my prayers today?

God, forgive me where I have been resentful, selfish, dishonest, or afraid today. Help me not to keep anything to myself, but to discuss it openly with another person. Show me where I owe an apology and help me make it, and help me to be kind and loving to all people. Use me in the mainstream of life, and remove worry, remorse, and morbid reflection that I may be of service to others. Amen.

When I retire at night...   /   /

Chronology of today's events:

Was I resentful?
    1. *Who/what*   3. *Affects*

    2. *Cause*   4. *My part*

Was I selfish?

Was I dishonest?

Was I afraid?

Do I owe an apology?

What have I wrongly kept secret?

Was I kind and loving toward all?

What could I have done better?

How did faith or fear rule my actions today?

Today I gave of my time ____, talent ____, treasure ____, and touch ____.

Who did I help today?

What am I grateful for today?

Who needs my prayers today?

God, forgive me where I have been resentful, selfish, dishonest, or afraid today. Help me not to keep anything to myself, but to discuss it openly with another person. Show me where I owe an apology and help me make it, and help me to be kind and loving to all people. Use me in the mainstream of life, and remove worry, remorse, and morbid reflection that I may be of service to others. Amen.

When I retire at night...   /   /

Chronology of today's events:

Was I resentful?
    1. *Who/what*   3. *Affects*

    2. *Cause*   4. *My part*

Was I selfish?

Was I dishonest?

Was I afraid?

Do I owe an apology?

What have I wrongly kept secret?

Was I kind and loving toward all?

What could I have done better?

How did faith or fear rule my actions today?

Today I gave of my time ___, talent ___, treasure ___, and touch ___.

Who did I help today?

What am I grateful for today?

Who needs my prayers today?

God, forgive me where I have been resentful, selfish, dishonest, or afraid today. Help me not to keep anything to myself, but to discuss it openly with another person. Show me where I owe an apology and help me make it, and help me to be kind and loving to all people. Use me in the mainstream of life, and remove worry, remorse, and morbid reflection that I may be of service to others. Amen.

When I retire at night...   /   /

Chronology of today's events:

Was I resentful?
    1. *Who/what*   3. *Affects*

    2. *Cause*   4. *My part*

Was I selfish?

Was I dishonest?

Was I afraid?

Do I owe an apology?

What have I wrongly kept secret?

Was I kind and loving toward all?

What could I have done better?

How did faith or fear rule my actions today?

Today I gave of my time ___, talent ___, treasure ___, and touch ___.

Who did I help today?

What am I grateful for today?

Who needs my prayers today?

God, forgive me where I have been resentful, selfish, dishonest, or afraid today. Help me not to keep anything to myself, but to discuss it openly with another person. Show me where I owe an apology and help me make it, and help me to be kind and loving to all people. Use me in the mainstream of life, and remove worry, remorse, and morbid reflection that I may be of service to others. Amen.

When I retire at night...   /   /

Chronology of today's events:

Was I resentful?
    1. *Who/what*   3. *Affects*

    2. *Cause*   4. *My part*

Was I selfish?

Was I dishonest?

Was I afraid?

Do I owe an apology?

What have I wrongly kept secret?

Was I kind and loving toward all?

What could I have done better?

How did faith or fear rule my actions today?

Today I gave of my time ___, talent ___, treasure ___, and touch ___.

Who did I help today?

What am I grateful for today?

Who needs my prayers today?

God, forgive me where I have been resentful, selfish, dishonest, or afraid today. Help me not to keep anything to myself, but to discuss it openly with another person. Show me where I owe an apology and help me make it, and help me to be kind and loving to all people. Use me in the mainstream of life, and remove worry, remorse, and morbid reflection that I may be of service to others. Amen.

When I retire at night...   /   /

Chronology of today's events:

Was I resentful?
    1. Who/what   *3. Affects*

    2. Cause   *4. My part*

Was I selfish?

Was I dishonest?

Was I afraid?

Do I owe an apology?

What have I wrongly kept secret?

Was I kind and loving toward all?

What could I have done better?

How did faith or fear rule my actions today?

Today I gave of my time ___, talent ___, treasure ___, and touch ___.

Who did I help today?

What am I grateful for today?

Who needs my prayers today?

God, forgive me where I have been resentful, selfish, dishonest, or afraid today. Help me not to keep anything to myself, but to discuss it openly with another person. Show me where I owe an apology and help me make it, and help me to be kind and loving to all people. Use me in the mainstream of life, and remove worry, remorse, and morbid reflection that I may be of service to others. Amen.

When I retire at night...   /   /

Chronology of today's events:

Was I resentful?
    1. *Who/what*   3.   *Affects*

    2. *Cause*   4.   *My part*

Was I selfish?

Was I dishonest?

Was I afraid?

Do I owe an apology?

What have I wrongly kept secret?

Was I kind and loving toward all?

What could I have done better?

How did faith or fear rule my actions today?

Today I gave of my time ___, talent ___, treasure ___, and touch ___.

Who did I help today?

What am I grateful for today?

Who needs my prayers today?

God, forgive me where I have been resentful, selfish, dishonest, or afraid today. Help me not to keep anything to myself, but to discuss it openly with another person. Show me where I owe an apology and help me make it, and help me to be kind and loving to all people. Use me in the mainstream of life, and remove worry, remorse, and morbid reflection that I may be of service to others. Amen.

When I retire at night...   /   /

Chronology of today's events:

Was I resentful?
    1. *Who/what*   3. *Affects*

    2. *Cause*   4. *My part*

Was I selfish?

Was I dishonest?

Was I afraid?

Do I owe an apology?

What have I wrongly kept secret?

Was I kind and loving toward all?

What could I have done better?

How did faith or fear rule my actions today?

Today I gave of my time ___, talent ___, treasure ___, and touch ___.

Who did I help today?

What am I grateful for today?

Who needs my prayers today?

God, forgive me where I have been resentful, selfish, dishonest, or afraid today. Help me not to keep anything to myself, but to discuss it openly with another person. Show me where I owe an apology and help me make it, and help me to be kind and loving to all people. Use me in the mainstream of life, and remove worry, remorse, and morbid reflection that I may be of service to others. Amen.

When I retire at night...   /   /

Chronology of today's events:

Was I resentful?
    1. *Who/what*   3. *Affects*

    2. *Cause*   4. *My part*

Was I selfish?

Was I dishonest?

Was I afraid?

Do I owe an apology?

What have I wrongly kept secret?

Was I kind and loving toward all?

What could I have done better?

How did faith or fear rule my actions today?

Today I gave of my time ___, talent ___, treasure ___, and touch ___.

Who did I help today?

What am I grateful for today?

Who needs my prayers today?

God, forgive me where I have been resentful, selfish, dishonest, or afraid today. Help me not to keep anything to myself, but to discuss it openly with another person. Show me where I owe an apology and help me make it, and help me to be kind and loving to all people. Use me in the mainstream of life, and remove worry, remorse, and morbid reflection that I may be of service to others. Amen.

When I retire at night...   /   /

Chronology of today's events:

Was I resentful?
    1. Who/what
    2. Cause
    3. Affects
    4. My part

Was I selfish?

Was I dishonest?

Was I afraid?

Do I owe an apology?

What have I wrongly kept secret?

Was I kind and loving toward all?

What could I have done better?

How did faith or fear rule my actions today?

Today I gave of my time ___, talent ___, treasure ___, and touch ___.

Who did I help today?

What am I grateful for today?

Who needs my prayers today?

God, forgive me where I have been resentful, selfish, dishonest, or afraid today. Help me not to keep anything to myself, but to discuss it openly with another person. Show me where I owe an apology and help me make it, and help me to be kind and loving to all people. Use me in the mainstream of life, and remove worry, remorse, and morbid reflection that I may be of service to others. Amen.

When I retire at night...   /   /

Chronology of today's events:

Was I resentful?
    1. *Who/what*   3. *Affects*

    2. *Cause*   4. *My part*

Was I selfish?

Was I dishonest?

Was I afraid?

Do I owe an apology?

What have I wrongly kept secret?

Was I kind and loving toward all?

What could I have done better?

How did faith or fear rule my actions today?

Today I gave of my time ___, talent ___, treasure ___, and touch ___.

Who did I help today?

What am I grateful for today?

Who needs my prayers today?

God, forgive me where I have been resentful, selfish, dishonest, or afraid today. Help me not to keep anything to myself, but to discuss it openly with another person. Show me where I owe an apology and help me make it, and help me to be kind and loving to all people. Use me in the mainstream of life, and remove worry, remorse, and morbid reflection that I may be of service to others. Amen.

When I retire at night...   /   /

Chronology of today's events:

Was I resentful?
    1. *Who/what*   3.   *Affects*

    2. *Cause*   4.   *My part*

Was I selfish?

Was I dishonest?

Was I afraid?

Do I owe an apology?

What have I wrongly kept secret?

Was I kind and loving toward all?

What could I have done better?

How did faith or fear rule my actions today?

Today I gave of my time ___, talent ___, treasure ___, and touch ___.

Who did I help today?

What am I grateful for today?

Who needs my prayers today?

God, forgive me where I have been resentful, selfish, dishonest, or afraid today. Help me not to keep anything to myself, but to discuss it openly with another person. Show me where I owe an apology and help me make it, and help me to be kind and loving to all people. Use me in the mainstream of life, and remove worry, remorse, and morbid reflection that I may be of service to others. Amen.

When I retire at night...   /   /

Chronology of today's events:

Was I resentful?
    1. *Who/what*   3. *Affects*

    2. *Cause*   4. *My part*

Was I selfish?

Was I dishonest?

Was I afraid?

Do I owe an apology?

What have I wrongly kept secret?

Was I kind and loving toward all?

What could I have done better?

How did faith or fear rule my actions today?

Today I gave of my time ___, talent ___, treasure ___, and touch ___.

Who did I help today?

What am I grateful for today?

Who needs my prayers today?

God, forgive me where I have been resentful, selfish, dishonest, or afraid today. Help me not to keep anything to myself, but to discuss it openly with another person. Show me where I owe an apology and help me make it, and help me to be kind and loving to all people. Use me in the mainstream of life, and remove worry, remorse, and morbid reflection that I may be of service to others. Amen.

When I retire at night...   /   /

Chronology of today's events:

Was I resentful?
    1. Who/what   3. Affects

    2. Cause   4. My part

Was I selfish?

Was I dishonest?

Was I afraid?

Do I owe an apology?

What have I wrongly kept secret?

Was I kind and loving toward all?

What could I have done better?

How did faith or fear rule my actions today?

Today I gave of my time ___, talent ___, treasure ___, and touch ___.

Who did I help today?

What am I grateful for today?

Who needs my prayers today?

God, forgive me where I have been resentful, selfish, dishonest, or afraid today. Help me not to keep anything to myself, but to discuss it openly with another person. Show me where I owe an apology and help me make it, and help me to be kind and loving to all people. Use me in the mainstream of life, and remove worry, remorse, and morbid reflection that I may be of service to others. Amen.

When I retire at night...   /   /

Chronology of today's events:

Was I resentful?
    1. *Who/what*   3. *Affects*

    2. *Cause*   4. *My part*

Was I selfish?

Was I dishonest?

Was I afraid?

Do I owe an apology?

What have I wrongly kept secret?

Was I kind and loving toward all?

What could I have done better?

How did faith or fear rule my actions today?

Today I gave of my time ___, talent ___, treasure ___, and touch ___.

Who did I help today?

What am I grateful for today?

Who needs my prayers today?

God, forgive me where I have been resentful, selfish, dishonest, or afraid today. Help me not to keep anything to myself, but to discuss it openly with another person. Show me where I owe an apology and help me make it, and help me to be kind and loving to all people. Use me in the mainstream of life, and remove worry, remorse, and morbid reflection that I may be of service to others. Amen.

When I retire at night...   /   /

Chronology of today's events:

Was I resentful?
    1. *Who/what*   3. *Affects*

    2. *Cause*   4. *My part*

Was I selfish?

Was I dishonest?

Was I afraid?

Do I owe an apology?

What have I wrongly kept secret?

Was I kind and loving toward all?

What could I have done better?

How did faith or fear rule my actions today?

Today I gave of my time ___, talent ___, treasure ___, and touch ___.

Who did I help today?

What am I grateful for today?

Who needs my prayers today?

God, forgive me where I have been resentful, selfish, dishonest, or afraid today. Help me not to keep anything to myself, but to discuss it openly with another person. Show me where I owe an apology and help me make it, and help me to be kind and loving to all people. Use me in the mainstream of life, and remove worry, remorse, and morbid reflection that I may be of service to others. Amen.

When I retire at night...   /   /

Chronology of today's events:

Was I resentful?
    1. *Who/what*   3. *Affects*

    2. *Cause*   4. *My part*

Was I selfish?

Was I dishonest?

Was I afraid?

Do I owe an apology?

What have I wrongly kept secret?

Was I kind and loving toward all?

What could I have done better?

How did faith or fear rule my actions today?

Today I gave of my time ___, talent ___, treasure ___, and touch ___.

Who did I help today?

What am I grateful for today?

Who needs my prayers today?

God, forgive me where I have been resentful, selfish, dishonest, or afraid today. Help me not to keep anything to myself, but to discuss it openly with another person. Show me where I owe an apology and help me make it, and help me to be kind and loving to all people. Use me in the mainstream of life, and remove worry, remorse, and morbid reflection that I may be of service to others. Amen.

When I retire at night...   /   /

Chronology of today's events:

Was I resentful?
    1. *Who/what*　　　　　　3.　*Affects*

    2. *Cause*　　　　　　　　4.　*My part*

Was I selfish?

Was I dishonest?

Was I afraid?

Do I owe an apology?

What have I wrongly kept secret?

Was I kind and loving toward all?

What could I have done better?

How did faith or fear rule my actions today?

Today I gave of my time ___, talent ___, treasure ___, and touch ___.

Who did I help today?

What am I grateful for today?

Who needs my prayers today?

God, forgive me where I have been resentful, selfish, dishonest, or afraid today. Help me not to keep anything to myself, but to discuss it openly with another person. Show me where I owe an apology and help me make it, and help me to be kind and loving to all people. Use me in the mainstream of life, and remove worry, remorse, and morbid reflection that I may be of service to others. Amen.

When I retire at night...   /   /

Chronology of today's events:

Was I resentful?
    1. *Who/what*   3. *Affects*

    2. *Cause*   4. *My part*

Was I selfish?

Was I dishonest?

Was I afraid?

Do I owe an apology?

What have I wrongly kept secret?

Was I kind and loving toward all?

What could I have done better?

How did faith or fear rule my actions today?

Today I gave of my time ___, talent ___, treasure ___, and touch ___.

Who did I help today?

What am I grateful for today?

Who needs my prayers today?

God, forgive me where I have been resentful, selfish, dishonest, or afraid today. Help me not to keep anything to myself, but to discuss it openly with another person. Show me where I owe an apology and help me make it, and help me to be kind and loving to all people. Use me in the mainstream of life, and remove worry, remorse, and morbid reflection that I may be of service to others. Amen.

When I retire at night...   /   /

Chronology of today's events:

Was I resentful?
    1. Who/what   3. Affects

    2. Cause   4. My part

Was I selfish?

Was I dishonest?

Was I afraid?

Do I owe an apology?

What have I wrongly kept secret?

Was I kind and loving toward all?

What could I have done better?

How did faith or fear rule my actions today?

Today I gave of my time ___, talent ___, treasure ___, and touch ___.

Who did I help today?

What am I grateful for today?

Who needs my prayers today?

God, forgive me where I have been resentful, selfish, dishonest, or afraid today. Help me not to keep anything to myself, but to discuss it openly with another person. Show me where I owe an apology and help me make it, and help me to be kind and loving to all people. Use me in the mainstream of life, and remove worry, remorse, and morbid reflection that I may be of service to others. Amen.

When I retire at night...   /   /

Chronology of today's events:

Was I resentful?

    1. *Who/what*   3. *Affects*

    2. *Cause*   4. *My part*

Was I selfish?

Was I dishonest?

Was I afraid?

Do I owe an apology?

What have I wrongly kept secret?

Was I kind and loving toward all?

What could I have done better?

How did faith or fear rule my actions today?

Today I gave of my time ___, talent ___, treasure ___, and touch ___.

Who did I help today?

What am I grateful for today?

Who needs my prayers today?

God, forgive me where I have been resentful, selfish, dishonest, or afraid today. Help me not to keep anything to myself, but to discuss it openly with another person. Show me where I owe an apology and help me make it, and help me to be kind and loving to all people. Use me in the mainstream of life, and remove worry, remorse, and morbid reflection that I may be of service to others. Amen.

When I retire at night...   /   /

Chronology of today's events:

Was I resentful?
    1. *Who/what*   3. *Affects*

    2. *Cause*   4. *My part*

Was I selfish?

Was I dishonest?

Was I afraid?

Do I owe an apology?

What have I wrongly kept secret?

Was I kind and loving toward all?

What could I have done better?

How did faith or fear rule my actions today?

Today I gave of my time ___, talent ___, treasure ___, and touch ___.

Who did I help today?

What am I grateful for today?

Who needs my prayers today?

God, forgive me where I have been resentful, selfish, dishonest, or afraid today. Help me not to keep anything to myself, but to discuss it openly with another person. Show me where I owe an apology and help me make it, and help me to be kind and loving to all people. Use me in the mainstream of life, and remove worry, remorse, and morbid reflection that I may be of service to others. Amen.

When I retire at night...   /   /

Chronology of today's events:

Was I resentful?
    1. *Who/what*   3. *Affects*

    2. *Cause*   4. *My part*

Was I selfish?

Was I dishonest?

Was I afraid?

Do I owe an apology?

What have I wrongly kept secret?

Was I kind and loving toward all?

What could I have done better?

How did faith or fear rule my actions today?

Today I gave of my time ___, talent ___, treasure ___, and touch ___.

Who did I help today?

What am I grateful for today?

Who needs my prayers today?

God, forgive me where I have been resentful, selfish, dishonest, or afraid today. Help me not to keep anything to myself, but to discuss it openly with another person. Show me where I owe an apology and help me make it, and help me to be kind and loving to all people. Use me in the mainstream of life, and remove worry, remorse, and morbid reflection that I may be of service to others. Amen.

When I retire at night...   /   /

Chronology of today's events:

Was I resentful?
    1. *Who/what*   3.   *Affects*

    2. *Cause*   4.   *My part*

Was I selfish?

Was I dishonest?

Was I afraid?

Do I owe an apology?

What have I wrongly kept secret?

Was I kind and loving toward all?

What could I have done better?

How did faith or fear rule my actions today?

Today I gave of my time ___, talent ___, treasure ___, and touch ___.

Who did I help today?

What am I grateful for today?

Who needs my prayers today?

God, forgive me where I have been resentful, selfish, dishonest, or afraid today. Help me not to keep anything to myself, but to discuss it openly with another person. Show me where I owe an apology and help me make it, and help me to be kind and loving to all people. Use me in the mainstream of life, and remove worry, remorse, and morbid reflection that I may be of service to others. Amen.

When I retire at night...   /   /

Chronology of today's events:

Was I resentful?
    1. *Who/what*　　　　　　　3. *Affects*

    2. *Cause*　　　　　　　　　4. *My part*

Was I selfish?

Was I dishonest?

Was I afraid?

Do I owe an apology?

What have I wrongly kept secret?

Was I kind and loving toward all?

What could I have done better?

How did faith or fear rule my actions today?

Today I gave of my time ___, talent ___, treasure ___, and touch ___.

Who did I help today?

What am I grateful for today?

Who needs my prayers today?

God, forgive me where I have been resentful, selfish, dishonest, or afraid today. Help me not to keep anything to myself, but to discuss it openly with another person. Show me where I owe an apology and help me make it, and help me to be kind and loving to all people. Use me in the mainstream of life, and remove worry, remorse, and morbid reflection that I may be of service to others. Amen.

When I retire at night...   /   /

Chronology of today's events:

Was I resentful?
    1. Who/what   3. Affects

    2. Cause   4. My part

Was I selfish?

Was I dishonest?

Was I afraid?

Do I owe an apology?

What have I wrongly kept secret?

Was I kind and loving toward all?

What could I have done better?

How did faith or fear rule my actions today?

Today I gave of my time ___, talent ___, treasure ___, and touch ___.

Who did I help today?

What am I grateful for today?

Who needs my prayers today?

God, forgive me where I have been resentful, selfish, dishonest, or afraid today. Help me not to keep anything to myself, but to discuss it openly with another person. Show me where I owe an apology and help me make it, and help me to be kind and loving to all people. Use me in the mainstream of life, and remove worry, remorse, and morbid reflection that I may be of service to others. Amen.

When I retire at night...   /   /

Chronology of today's events:

Was I resentful?
    1. Who/what   3. Affects

    2. Cause   4. My part

Was I selfish?

Was I dishonest?

Was I afraid?

Do I owe an apology?

What have I wrongly kept secret?

Was I kind and loving toward all?

What could I have done better?

How did faith or fear rule my actions today?

Today I gave of my time ___, talent ___, treasure ___, and touch ___.

Who did I help today?

What am I grateful for today?

Who needs my prayers today?

God, forgive me where I have been resentful, selfish, dishonest, or afraid today. Help me not to keep anything to myself, but to discuss it openly with another person. Show me where I owe an apology and help me make it, and help me to be kind and loving to all people. Use me in the mainstream of life, and remove worry, remorse, and morbid reflection that I may be of service to others. Amen.

When I retire at night...   /   /

Chronology of today's events:

Was I resentful?
    1. Who/what   *3. Affects*

    2. Cause   *4. My part*

Was I selfish?

Was I dishonest?

Was I afraid?

Do I owe an apology?

What have I wrongly kept secret?

Was I kind and loving toward all?

What could I have done better?

How did faith or fear rule my actions today?

Today I gave of my time ___, talent ___, treasure ___, and touch ___.

Who did I help today?

What am I grateful for today?

Who needs my prayers today?

God, forgive me where I have been resentful, selfish, dishonest, or afraid today. Help me not to keep anything to myself, but to discuss it openly with another person. Show me where I owe an apology and help me make it, and help me to be kind and loving to all people. Use me in the mainstream of life, and remove worry, remorse, and morbid reflection that I may be of service to others. Amen.

When I retire at night...   /   /

Chronology of today's events:

Was I resentful?
    1. *Who/what*   3. *Affects*

    2. *Cause*   4. *My part*

Was I selfish?

Was I dishonest?

Was I afraid?

Do I owe an apology?

What have I wrongly kept secret?

Was I kind and loving toward all?

What could I have done better?

How did faith or fear rule my actions today?

Today I gave of my time ___, talent ___, treasure ___, and touch ___.

Who did I help today?

What am I grateful for today?

Who needs my prayers today?

God, forgive me where I have been resentful, selfish, dishonest, or afraid today. Help me not to keep anything to myself, but to discuss it openly with another person. Show me where I owe an apology and help me make it, and help me to be kind and loving to all people. Use me in the mainstream of life, and remove worry, remorse, and morbid reflection that I may be of service to others. Amen.

When I retire at night...   /   /

Chronology of today's events:

Was I resentful?
    1. *Who/what*   3. *Affects*

    2. *Cause*   4. *My part*

Was I selfish?

Was I dishonest?

Was I afraid?

Do I owe an apology?

What have I wrongly kept secret?

Was I kind and loving toward all?

What could I have done better?

How did faith or fear rule my actions today?

Today I gave of my time ___, talent ___, treasure ___, and touch ___.

Who did I help today?

What am I grateful for today?

Who needs my prayers today?

God, forgive me where I have been resentful, selfish, dishonest, or afraid today. Help me not to keep anything to myself, but to discuss it openly with another person. Show me where I owe an apology and help me make it, and help me to be kind and loving to all people. Use me in the mainstream of life, and remove worry, remorse, and morbid reflection that I may be of service to others. Amen.

When I retire at night…   /   /

Chronology of today's events:

Was I resentful?
  1. *Who/what*   3. *Affects*
  2. *Cause*   4. *My part*

Was I selfish?

Was I dishonest?

Was I afraid?

Do I owe an apology?

What have I wrongly kept secret?

Was I kind and loving toward all?

What could I have done better?

How did faith or fear rule my actions today?

Today I gave of my time ___, talent ___, treasure ___, and touch ___.

Who did I help today?

What am I grateful for today?

Who needs my prayers today?

God, forgive me where I have been resentful, selfish, dishonest, or afraid today. Help me not to keep anything to myself, but to discuss it openly with another person. Show me where I owe an apology and help me make it, and help me to be kind and loving to all people. Use me in the mainstream of life, and remove worry, remorse, and morbid reflection that I may be of service to others. Amen.

When I retire at night...   /   /

Chronology of today's events:

Was I resentful?
    1. Who/what   3. Affects

    2. Cause   4. My part

Was I selfish?

Was I dishonest?

Was I afraid?

Do I owe an apology?

What have I wrongly kept secret?

Was I kind and loving toward all?

What could I have done better?

How did faith or fear rule my actions today?

Today I gave of my time ___, talent ___, treasure ___, and touch ___.

Who did I help today?

What am I grateful for today?

Who needs my prayers today?

God, forgive me where I have been resentful, selfish, dishonest, or afraid today. Help me not to keep anything to myself, but to discuss it openly with another person. Show me where I owe an apology and help me make it, and help me to be kind and loving to all people. Use me in the mainstream of life, and remove worry, remorse, and morbid reflection that I may be of service to others. Amen.

When I retire at night...   /   /

Chronology of today's events:

Was I resentful?
    1. Who/what   3. Affects

    2. Cause   4. My part

Was I selfish?

Was I dishonest?

Was I afraid?

Do I owe an apology?

What have I wrongly kept secret?

Was I kind and loving toward all?

What could I have done better?

How did faith or fear rule my actions today?

Today I gave of my time ___, talent ___, treasure ___, and touch ___.

Who did I help today?

What am I grateful for today?

Who needs my prayers today?

God, forgive me where I have been resentful, selfish, dishonest, or afraid today. Help me not to keep anything to myself, but to discuss it openly with another person. Show me where I owe an apology and help me make it, and help me to be kind and loving to all people. Use me in the mainstream of life, and remove worry, remorse, and morbid reflection that I may be of service to others. Amen.

When I retire at night...   /   /

Chronology of today's events:

Was I resentful?
    1. Who/what   *3. Affects*

    2. Cause   *4. My part*

Was I selfish?

Was I dishonest?

Was I afraid?

Do I owe an apology?

What have I wrongly kept secret?

Was I kind and loving toward all?

What could I have done better?

How did faith or fear rule my actions today?

Today I gave of my time ___, talent ___, treasure ___, and touch ___.

Who did I help today?

What am I grateful for today?

Who needs my prayers today?

God, forgive me where I have been resentful, selfish, dishonest, or afraid today. Help me not to keep anything to myself, but to discuss it openly with another person. Show me where I owe an apology and help me make it, and help me to be kind and loving to all people. Use me in the mainstream of life, and remove worry, remorse, and morbid reflection that I may be of service to others. Amen.

When I retire at night...   /   /

Chronology of today's events:

Was I resentful?
1. *Who/what*
2. *Cause*
3. *Affects*
4. *My part*

Was I selfish?

Was I dishonest?

Was I afraid?

Do I owe an apology?

What have I wrongly kept secret?

Was I kind and loving toward all?

What could I have done better?

How did faith or fear rule my actions today?

Today I gave of my time ___, talent ___, treasure ___, and touch ___.

Who did I help today?

What am I grateful for today?

Who needs my prayers today?

God, forgive me where I have been resentful, selfish, dishonest, or afraid today. Help me not to keep anything to myself, but to discuss it openly with another person. Show me where I owe an apology and help me make it, and help me to be kind and loving to all people. Use me in the mainstream of life, and remove worry, remorse, and morbid reflection that I may be of service to others. Amen.

When I retire at night...   /   /

Chronology of today's events:

Was I resentful?
    1. *Who/what*   3. *Affects*

    2. *Cause*   4. *My part*

Was I selfish?

Was I dishonest?

Was I afraid?

Do I owe an apology?

What have I wrongly kept secret?

Was I kind and loving toward all?

What could I have done better?

How did faith or fear rule my actions today?

Today I gave of my time ___, talent ___, treasure ___, and touch ___.

Who did I help today?

What am I grateful for today?

Who needs my prayers today?

God, forgive me where I have been resentful, selfish, dishonest, or afraid today. Help me not to keep anything to myself, but to discuss it openly with another person. Show me where I owe an apology and help me make it, and help me to be kind and loving to all people. Use me in the mainstream of life, and remove worry, remorse, and morbid reflection that I may be of service to others. Amen.

When I retire at night...   /   /

Chronology of today's events:

Was I resentful?
    1. *Who/what*   3. *Affects*

    2. *Cause*   4. *My part*

Was I selfish?

Was I dishonest?

Was I afraid?

Do I owe an apology?

What have I wrongly kept secret?

Was I kind and loving toward all?

What could I have done better?

How did faith or fear rule my actions today?

Today I gave of my time ___, talent ___, treasure ___, and touch ___.

Who did I help today?

What am I grateful for today?

Who needs my prayers today?

God, forgive me where I have been resentful, selfish, dishonest, or afraid today. Help me not to keep anything to myself, but to discuss it openly with another person. Show me where I owe an apology and help me make it, and help me to be kind and loving to all people. Use me in the mainstream of life, and remove worry, remorse, and morbid reflection that I may be of service to others. Amen.

When I retire at night...   /   /

Chronology of today's events:

Was I resentful?
    1. Who/what   3. Affects

    2. Cause   4. My part

Was I selfish?

Was I dishonest?

Was I afraid?

Do I owe an apology?

What have I wrongly kept secret?

Was I kind and loving toward all?

What could I have done better?

How did faith or fear rule my actions today?

Today I gave of my time ___, talent ___, treasure ___, and touch ___.

Who did I help today?

What am I grateful for today?

Who needs my prayers today?

God, forgive me where I have been resentful, selfish, dishonest, or afraid today. Help me not to keep anything to myself, but to discuss it openly with another person. Show me where I owe an apology and help me make it, and help me to be kind and loving to all people. Use me in the mainstream of life, and remove worry, remorse, and morbid reflection that I may be of service to others. Amen.

When I retire at night...   /   /

Chronology of today's events:

Was I resentful?
    1. *Who/what*   3. *Affects*

    2. *Cause*   4. *My part*

Was I selfish?

Was I dishonest?

Was I afraid?

Do I owe an apology?

What have I wrongly kept secret?

Was I kind and loving toward all?

What could I have done better?

How did faith or fear rule my actions today?

Today I gave of my time ___, talent ___, treasure ___, and touch ___.

Who did I help today?

What am I grateful for today?

Who needs my prayers today?

God, forgive me where I have been resentful, selfish, dishonest, or afraid today. Help me not to keep anything to myself, but to discuss it openly with another person. Show me where I owe an apology and help me make it, and help me to be kind and loving to all people. Use me in the mainstream of life, and remove worry, remorse, and morbid reflection that I may be of service to others. Amen.

When I retire at night...   /   /

Chronology of today's events:

Was I resentful?
  1. *Who/what*   3. *Affects*
  2. *Cause*   4. *My part*

Was I selfish?

Was I dishonest?

Was I afraid?

Do I owe an apology?

What have I wrongly kept secret?

Was I kind and loving toward all?

What could I have done better?

How did faith or fear rule my actions today?

Today I gave of my time ____, talent ____, treasure ____, and touch ____.

Who did I help today?

What am I grateful for today?

Who needs my prayers today?

God, forgive me where I have been resentful, selfish, dishonest, or afraid today. Help me not to keep anything to myself, but to discuss it openly with another person. Show me where I owe an apology and help me make it, and help me to be kind and loving to all people. Use me in the mainstream of life, and remove worry, remorse, and morbid reflection that I may be of service to others. Amen.

When I retire at night...   /   /

Chronology of today's events:

Was I resentful?
    1. *Who/what*   3. *Affects*

    2. *Cause*   4. *My part*

Was I selfish?

Was I dishonest?

Was I afraid?

Do I owe an apology?

What have I wrongly kept secret?

Was I kind and loving toward all?

What could I have done better?

How did faith or fear rule my actions today?

Today I gave of my time ___, talent ___, treasure ___, and touch ___.

Who did I help today?

What am I grateful for today?

Who needs my prayers today?

God, forgive me where I have been resentful, selfish, dishonest, or afraid today. Help me not to keep anything to myself, but to discuss it openly with another person. Show me where I owe an apology and help me make it, and help me to be kind and loving to all people. Use me in the mainstream of life, and remove worry, remorse, and morbid reflection that I may be of service to others. Amen.

When I retire at night...   /   /

Chronology of today's events:

Was I resentful?
   1. Who/what   3. Affects

   2. Cause   4. My part

Was I selfish?

Was I dishonest?

Was I afraid?

Do I owe an apology?

What have I wrongly kept secret?

Was I kind and loving toward all?

What could I have done better?

How did faith or fear rule my actions today?

Today I gave of my time ___, talent ___, treasure ___, and touch ___.

Who did I help today?

What am I grateful for today?

Who needs my prayers today?

God, forgive me where I have been resentful, selfish, dishonest, or afraid today. Help me not to keep anything to myself, but to discuss it openly with another person. Show me where I owe an apology and help me make it, and help me to be kind and loving to all people. Use me in the mainstream of life, and remove worry, remorse, and morbid reflection that I may be of service to others. Amen.

When I retire at night...   /   /

Chronology of today's events:

Was I resentful?
  1. *Who/what*
  2. *Cause*
  3. *Affects*
  4. *My part*

Was I selfish?

Was I dishonest?

Was I afraid?

Do I owe an apology?

What have I wrongly kept secret?

Was I kind and loving toward all?

What could I have done better?

How did faith or fear rule my actions today?

Today I gave of my time ___, talent ___, treasure ___, and touch ___.

Who did I help today?

What am I grateful for today?

Who needs my prayers today?

God, forgive me where I have been resentful, selfish, dishonest, or afraid today. Help me not to keep anything to myself, but to discuss it openly with another person. Show me where I owe an apology and help me make it, and help me to be kind and loving to all people. Use me in the mainstream of life, and remove worry, remorse, and morbid reflection that I may be of service to others. Amen.

When I retire at night...   /   /

Chronology of today's events:

Was I resentful?
    1. Who/what   3.   Affects

    2. Cause   4.   My part

Was I selfish?

Was I dishonest?

Was I afraid?

Do I owe an apology?

What have I wrongly kept secret?

Was I kind and loving toward all?

What could I have done better?

How did faith or fear rule my actions today?

Today I gave of my time ___, talent ___, treasure ___, and touch ___.

Who did I help today?

What am I grateful for today?

Who needs my prayers today?

God, forgive me where I have been resentful, selfish, dishonest, or afraid today. Help me not to keep anything to myself, but to discuss it openly with another person. Show me where I owe an apology and help me make it, and help me to be kind and loving to all people. Use me in the mainstream of life, and remove worry, remorse, and morbid reflection that I may be of service to others. Amen.

When I retire at night...   /   /

Chronology of today's events:

___

Was I resentful?
   1. Who/what   3. Affects

   2. Cause   4. My part

Was I selfish?

Was I dishonest?

Was I afraid?

Do I owe an apology?

What have I wrongly kept secret?

Was I kind and loving toward all?

What could I have done better?

How did faith or fear rule my actions today?

Today I gave of my time ___, talent ___, treasure ___, and touch ___.

Who did I help today?

What am I grateful for today?

Who needs my prayers today?

___

God, forgive me where I have been resentful, selfish, dishonest, or afraid today. Help me not to keep anything to myself, but to discuss it openly with another person. Show me where I owe an apology and help me make it, and help me to be kind and loving to all people. Use me in the mainstream of life, and remove worry, remorse, and morbid reflection that I may be of service to others. Amen.

When I retire at night...   /   /

Chronology of today's events:

Was I resentful?
    1. *Who/what*   3. *Affects*

    2. *Cause*   4. *My part*

Was I selfish?

Was I dishonest?

Was I afraid?

Do I owe an apology?

What have I wrongly kept secret?

Was I kind and loving toward all?

What could I have done better?

How did faith or fear rule my actions today?

Today I gave of my time ___, talent ___, treasure ___, and touch ___.

Who did I help today?

What am I grateful for today?

Who needs my prayers today?

God, forgive me where I have been resentful, selfish, dishonest, or afraid today. Help me not to keep anything to myself, but to discuss it openly with another person. Show me where I owe an apology and help me make it, and help me to be kind and loving to all people. Use me in the mainstream of life, and remove worry, remorse, and morbid reflection that I may be of service to others. Amen.

When I retire at night...   /   /

Chronology of today's events:

Was I resentful?
    1. *Who/what*   3. *Affects*

    2. *Cause*   4. *My part*

Was I selfish?

Was I dishonest?

Was I afraid?

Do I owe an apology?

What have I wrongly kept secret?

Was I kind and loving toward all?

What could I have done better?

How did faith or fear rule my actions today?

Today I gave of my time ___, talent ___, treasure ___, and touch ___.

Who did I help today?

What am I grateful for today?

Who needs my prayers today?

God, forgive me where I have been resentful, selfish, dishonest, or afraid today. Help me not to keep anything to myself, but to discuss it openly with another person. Show me where I owe an apology and help me make it, and help me to be kind and loving to all people. Use me in the mainstream of life, and remove worry, remorse, and morbid reflection that I may be of service to others. Amen.

When I retire at night...   /   /

Chronology of today's events:

Was I resentful?
    1. *Who/what*   3. *Affects*

    2. *Cause*   4. *My part*

Was I selfish?

Was I dishonest?

Was I afraid?

Do I owe an apology?

What have I wrongly kept secret?

Was I kind and loving toward all?

What could I have done better?

How did faith or fear rule my actions today?

Today I gave of my time ___, talent ___, treasure ___, and touch ___.

Who did I help today?

What am I grateful for today?

Who needs my prayers today?

God, forgive me where I have been resentful, selfish, dishonest, or afraid today. Help me not to keep anything to myself, but to discuss it openly with another person. Show me where I owe an apology and help me make it, and help me to be kind and loving to all people. Use me in the mainstream of life, and remove worry, remorse, and morbid reflection that I may be of service to others. Amen.

When I retire at night...   /   /

Chronology of today's events:

Was I resentful?
    1. *Who/what*   3. *Affects*

    2. *Cause*   4. *My part*

Was I selfish?

Was I dishonest?

Was I afraid?

Do I owe an apology?

What have I wrongly kept secret?

Was I kind and loving toward all?

What could I have done better?

How did faith or fear rule my actions today?

Today I gave of my time ___, talent ___, treasure ___, and touch ___.

Who did I help today?

What am I grateful for today?

Who needs my prayers today?

God, forgive me where I have been resentful, selfish, dishonest, or afraid today. Help me not to keep anything to myself, but to discuss it openly with another person. Show me where I owe an apology and help me make it, and help me to be kind and loving to all people. Use me in the mainstream of life, and remove worry, remorse, and morbid reflection that I may be of service to others. Amen.

When I retire at night...   /   /

Chronology of today's events:

_____

_____

Was I resentful?

    1. *Who/what*   3. *Affects*

    2. *Cause*   4. *My part*

Was I selfish?

Was I dishonest?

Was I afraid?

Do I owe an apology?

What have I wrongly kept secret?

Was I kind and loving toward all?

What could I have done better?

How did faith or fear rule my actions today?

Today I gave of my time ___, talent ___, treasure ___, and touch ___.

Who did I help today?

What am I grateful for today?

Who needs my prayers today?

God, forgive me where I have been resentful, selfish, dishonest, or afraid today. Help me not to keep anything to myself, but to discuss it openly with another person. Show me where I owe an apology and help me make it, and help me to be kind and loving to all people. Use me in the mainstream of life, and remove worry, remorse, and morbid reflection that I may be of service to others. Amen.

When I retire at night...   /   /

Chronology of today's events:

_____
_____
_____

Was I resentful?
    1. *Who/what*   3. *Affects*

    2. *Cause*   4. *My part*

Was I selfish?

Was I dishonest?

Was I afraid?

Do I owe an apology?

What have I wrongly kept secret?

Was I kind and loving toward all?

What could I have done better?

How did faith or fear rule my actions today?

Today I gave of my time ___, talent ___, treasure ___, and touch ___.

Who did I help today?

What am I grateful for today?

Who needs my prayers today?

God, forgive me where I have been resentful, selfish, dishonest, or afraid today. Help me not to keep anything to myself, but to discuss it openly with another person. Show me where I owe an apology and help me make it, and help me to be kind and loving to all people. Use me in the mainstream of life, and remove worry, remorse, and morbid reflection that I may be of service to others. Amen.

When I retire at night…   /   /

Chronology of today's events:

Was I resentful?
    1. *Who/what*   3. *Affects*

    2. *Cause*   4. *My part*

Was I selfish?

Was I dishonest?

Was I afraid?

Do I owe an apology?

What have I wrongly kept secret?

Was I kind and loving toward all?

What could I have done better?

How did faith or fear rule my actions today?

Today I gave of my time ___, talent ___, treasure ___, and touch ___.

Who did I help today?

What am I grateful for today?

Who needs my prayers today?

God, forgive me where I have been resentful, selfish, dishonest, or afraid today. Help me not to keep anything to myself, but to discuss it openly with another person. Show me where I owe an apology and help me make it, and help me to be kind and loving to all people. Use me in the mainstream of life, and remove worry, remorse, and morbid reflection that I may be of service to others. Amen.

When I retire at night...   /   /

Chronology of today's events:

Was I resentful?
- 1. *Who/what*
- 2. *Cause*
- 3. *Affects*
- 4. *My part*

Was I selfish?

Was I dishonest?

Was I afraid?

Do I owe an apology?

What have I wrongly kept secret?

Was I kind and loving toward all?

What could I have done better?

How did faith or fear rule my actions today?

Today I gave of my time ___, talent ___, treasure ___, and touch ___.

Who did I help today?

What am I grateful for today?

Who needs my prayers today?

God, forgive me where I have been resentful, selfish, dishonest, or afraid today. Help me not to keep anything to myself, but to discuss it openly with another person. Show me where I owe an apology and help me make it, and help me to be kind and loving to all people. Use me in the mainstream of life, and remove worry, remorse, and morbid reflection that I may be of service to others. Amen.

When I retire at night...   /   /

Chronology of today's events:

_____
_____
_____

Was I resentful?
    1. *Who/what*   3. *Affects*

    2. *Cause*   4. *My part*

Was I selfish?

Was I dishonest?

Was I afraid?

Do I owe an apology?

What have I wrongly kept secret?

Was I kind and loving toward all?

What could I have done better?

How did faith or fear rule my actions today?

Today I gave of my time ___, talent ___, treasure ___, and touch ___.

Who did I help today?

What am I grateful for today?

Who needs my prayers today?

God, forgive me where I have been resentful, selfish, dishonest, or afraid today. Help me not to keep anything to myself, but to discuss it openly with another person. Show me where I owe an apology and help me make it, and help me to be kind and loving to all people. Use me in the mainstream of life, and remove worry, remorse, and morbid reflection that I may be of service to others. Amen.

When I retire at night...   /   /

Chronology of today's events:

Was I resentful?
    1. *Who/what*　　　　　　　3. *Affects*

    2. *Cause*　　　　　　　　　4. *My part*

Was I selfish?

Was I dishonest?

Was I afraid?

Do I owe an apology?

What have I wrongly kept secret?

Was I kind and loving toward all?

What could I have done better?

How did faith or fear rule my actions today?

Today I gave of my time ___, talent ___, treasure ___, and touch ___.

Who did I help today?

What am I grateful for today?

Who needs my prayers today?

God, forgive me where I have been resentful, selfish, dishonest, or afraid today. Help me not to keep anything to myself, but to discuss it openly with another person. Show me where I owe an apology and help me make it, and help me to be kind and loving to all people. Use me in the mainstream of life, and remove worry, remorse, and morbid reflection that I may be of service to others. Amen.

When I retire at night...   /   /

Chronology of today's events:

Was I resentful?
    1. Who/what   3. Affects

    2. Cause   4. My part

Was I selfish?

Was I dishonest?

Was I afraid?

Do I owe an apology?

What have I wrongly kept secret?

Was I kind and loving toward all?

What could I have done better?

How did faith or fear rule my actions today?

Today I gave of my time ___, talent ___, treasure ___, and touch ___.

Who did I help today?

What am I grateful for today?

Who needs my prayers today?

God, forgive me where I have been resentful, selfish, dishonest, or afraid today. Help me not to keep anything to myself, but to discuss it openly with another person. Show me where I owe an apology and help me make it, and help me to be kind and loving to all people. Use me in the mainstream of life, and remove worry, remorse, and morbid reflection that I may be of service to others. Amen.

When I retire at night...   /   /

Chronology of today's events:

Was I resentful?
    1. *Who/what*　　　　　　　3. *Affects*

    2. *Cause*　　　　　　　　　4. *My part*

Was I selfish?

Was I dishonest?

Was I afraid?

Do I owe an apology?

What have I wrongly kept secret?

Was I kind and loving toward all?

What could I have done better?

How did faith or fear rule my actions today?

Today I gave of my time ___, talent ___, treasure ___, and touch ___.

Who did I help today?

What am I grateful for today?

Who needs my prayers today?

God, forgive me where I have been resentful, selfish, dishonest, or afraid today. Help me not to keep anything to myself, but to discuss it openly with another person. Show me where I owe an apology and help me make it, and help me to be kind and loving to all people. Use me in the mainstream of life, and remove worry, remorse, and morbid reflection that I may be of service to others. Amen.

When I retire at night...   /   /

Chronology of today's events:

Was I resentful?
    1. Who/what　　　　　　　　*3. Affects*

    2. Cause　　　　　　　　　　*4. My part*

Was I selfish?

Was I dishonest?

Was I afraid?

Do I owe an apology?

What have I wrongly kept secret?

Was I kind and loving toward all?

What could I have done better?

How did faith or fear rule my actions today?

Today I gave of my time ___, talent ___, treasure ___, and touch ___.

Who did I help today?

What am I grateful for today?

Who needs my prayers today?

God, forgive me where I have been resentful, selfish, dishonest, or afraid today. Help me not to keep anything to myself, but to discuss it openly with another person. Show me where I owe an apology and help me make it, and help me to be kind and loving to all people. Use me in the mainstream of life, and remove worry, remorse, and morbid reflection that I may be of service to others. Amen.

When I retire at night...   /   /

Chronology of today's events:

Was I resentful?

    1. *Who/what*   3. *Affects*

    2. *Cause*   4. *My part*

Was I selfish?

Was I dishonest?

Was I afraid?

Do I owe an apology?

What have I wrongly kept secret?

Was I kind and loving toward all?

What could I have done better?

How did faith or fear rule my actions today?

Today I gave of my time ___, talent ___, treasure ___, and touch ___.

Who did I help today?

What am I grateful for today?

Who needs my prayers today?

God, forgive me where I have been resentful, selfish, dishonest, or afraid today. Help me not to keep anything to myself, but to discuss it openly with another person. Show me where I owe an apology and help me make it, and help me to be kind and loving to all people. Use me in the mainstream of life, and remove worry, remorse, and morbid reflection that I may be of service to others. Amen.

When I retire at night...   /   /

Chronology of today's events:

Was I resentful?
    1. *Who/what*   3. *Affects*

    2. *Cause*   4. *My part*

Was I selfish?

Was I dishonest?

Was I afraid?

Do I owe an apology?

What have I wrongly kept secret?

Was I kind and loving toward all?

What could I have done better?

How did faith or fear rule my actions today?

Today I gave of my time ___, talent ___, treasure ___, and touch ___.

Who did I help today?

What am I grateful for today?

Who needs my prayers today?

God, forgive me where I have been resentful, selfish, dishonest, or afraid today. Help me not to keep anything to myself, but to discuss it openly with another person. Show me where I owe an apology and help me make it, and help me to be kind and loving to all people. Use me in the mainstream of life, and remove worry, remorse, and morbid reflection that I may be of service to others. Amen.

When I retire at night…   /   /

Chronology of today's events:

Was I resentful?
    1. *Who/what*   3. *Affects*

    2. *Cause*   4. *My part*

Was I selfish?

Was I dishonest?

Was I afraid?

Do I owe an apology?

What have I wrongly kept secret?

Was I kind and loving toward all?

What could I have done better?

How did faith or fear rule my actions today?

Today I gave of my time ___, talent ___, treasure ___, and touch ___.

Who did I help today?

What am I grateful for today?

Who needs my prayers today?

God, forgive me where I have been resentful, selfish, dishonest, or afraid today. Help me not to keep anything to myself, but to discuss it openly with another person. Show me where I owe an apology and help me make it, and help me to be kind and loving to all people. Use me in the mainstream of life, and remove worry, remorse, and morbid reflection that I may be of service to others. Amen.

When I retire at night...   /   /

Chronology of today's events:

Was I resentful?
    1. *Who/what*   3. *Affects*

    2. *Cause*   4. *My part*

Was I selfish?

Was I dishonest?

Was I afraid?

Do I owe an apology?

What have I wrongly kept secret?

Was I kind and loving toward all?

What could I have done better?

How did faith or fear rule my actions today?

Today I gave of my time ___, talent ___, treasure ___, and touch ___.

Who did I help today?

What am I grateful for today?

Who needs my prayers today?

God, forgive me where I have been resentful, selfish, dishonest, or afraid today. Help me not to keep anything to myself, but to discuss it openly with another person. Show me where I owe an apology and help me make it, and help me to be kind and loving to all people. Use me in the mainstream of life, and remove worry, remorse, and morbid reflection that I may be of service to others. Amen.

When I retire at night...   /   /

Chronology of today's events:

Was I resentful?

    1. Who/what   3. Affects

    2. Cause   4. My part

Was I selfish?

Was I dishonest?

Was I afraid?

Do I owe an apology?

What have I wrongly kept secret?

Was I kind and loving toward all?

What could I have done better?

How did faith or fear rule my actions today?

Today I gave of my time ___, talent ___, treasure ___, and touch ___.

Who did I help today?

What am I grateful for today?

Who needs my prayers today?

God, forgive me where I have been resentful, selfish, dishonest, or afraid today. Help me not to keep anything to myself, but to discuss it openly with another person. Show me where I owe an apology and help me make it, and help me to be kind and loving to all people. Use me in the mainstream of life, and remove worry, remorse, and morbid reflection that I may be of service to others. Amen.

When I retire at night...   /   /

Chronology of today's events:

Was I resentful?
    1. *Who/what*   3. *Affects*

    2. *Cause*   4. *My part*

Was I selfish?

Was I dishonest?

Was I afraid?

Do I owe an apology?

What have I wrongly kept secret?

Was I kind and loving toward all?

What could I have done better?

How did faith or fear rule my actions today?

Today I gave of my time ___, talent ___, treasure ___, and touch ___.

Who did I help today?

What am I grateful for today?

Who needs my prayers today?

God, forgive me where I have been resentful, selfish, dishonest, or afraid today. Help me not to keep anything to myself, but to discuss it openly with another person. Show me where I owe an apology and help me make it, and help me to be kind and loving to all people. Use me in the mainstream of life, and remove worry, remorse, and morbid reflection that I may be of service to others. Amen.

When I retire at night...   /   /

Chronology of today's events:

Was I resentful?
    1. *Who/what*   3. *Affects*

    2. *Cause*   4. *My part*

Was I selfish?

Was I dishonest?

Was I afraid?

Do I owe an apology?

What have I wrongly kept secret?

Was I kind and loving toward all?

What could I have done better?

How did faith or fear rule my actions today?

Today I gave of my time ___, talent ___, treasure ___, and touch ___.

Who did I help today?

What am I grateful for today?

Who needs my prayers today?

God, forgive me where I have been resentful, selfish, dishonest, or afraid today. Help me not to keep anything to myself, but to discuss it openly with another person. Show me where I owe an apology and help me make it, and help me to be kind and loving to all people. Use me in the mainstream of life, and remove worry, remorse, and morbid reflection that I may be of service to others. Amen.

When I retire at night...   /   /

Chronology of today's events:

Was I resentful?
    1. *Who / what*   3. *Affects*

    2. *Cause*   4. *My part*

Was I selfish?

Was I dishonest?

Was I afraid?

Do I owe an apology?

What have I wrongly kept secret?

Was I kind and loving toward all?

What could I have done better?

How did faith or fear rule my actions today?

Today I gave of my time ___, talent ___, treasure ___, and touch ___.

Who did I help today?

What am I grateful for today?

Who needs my prayers today?

God, forgive me where I have been resentful, selfish, dishonest, or afraid today. Help me not to keep anything to myself, but to discuss it openly with another person. Show me where I owe an apology and help me make it, and help me to be kind and loving to all people. Use me in the mainstream of life, and remove worry, remorse, and morbid reflection that I may be of service to others. Amen.

When I retire at night…   /   /

Chronology of today's events:

Was I resentful?
    1. *Who/what*   3. *Affects*

    2. *Cause*   4. *My part*

Was I selfish?

Was I dishonest?

Was I afraid?

Do I owe an apology?

What have I wrongly kept secret?

Was I kind and loving toward all?

What could I have done better?

How did faith or fear rule my actions today?

Today I gave of my time ___, talent ___, treasure ___, and touch ___.

Who did I help today?

What am I grateful for today?

Who needs my prayers today?

God, forgive me where I have been resentful, selfish, dishonest, or afraid today. Help me not to keep anything to myself, but to discuss it openly with another person. Show me where I owe an apology and help me make it, and help me to be kind and loving to all people. Use me in the mainstream of life, and remove worry, remorse, and morbid reflection that I may be of service to others. Amen.

When I retire at night...   /   /

Chronology of today's events:

Was I resentful?
    1. Who/what　　　　　　　3. Affects

    2. Cause　　　　　　　　　4. My part

Was I selfish?

Was I dishonest?

Was I afraid?

Do I owe an apology?

What have I wrongly kept secret?

Was I kind and loving toward all?

What could I have done better?

How did faith or fear rule my actions today?

Today I gave of my time ___, talent ___, treasure ___, and touch ___.

Who did I help today?

What am I grateful for today?

Who needs my prayers today?

God, forgive me where I have been resentful, selfish, dishonest, or afraid today. Help me not to keep anything to myself, but to discuss it openly with another person. Show me where I owe an apology and help me make it, and help me to be kind and loving to all people. Use me in the mainstream of life, and remove worry, remorse, and morbid reflection that I may be of service to others. Amen.

When I retire at night...   /   /

Chronology of today's events:

Was I resentful?
    1. Who/what   3. Affects

    2. Cause   4. My part

Was I selfish?

Was I dishonest?

Was I afraid?

Do I owe an apology?

What have I wrongly kept secret?

Was I kind and loving toward all?

What could I have done better?

How did faith or fear rule my actions today?

Today I gave of my time ___, talent ___, treasure ___, and touch ___.

Who did I help today?

What am I grateful for today?

Who needs my prayers today?

God, forgive me where I have been resentful, selfish, dishonest, or afraid today. Help me not to keep anything to myself, but to discuss it openly with another person. Show me where I owe an apology and help me make it, and help me to be kind and loving to all people. Use me in the mainstream of life, and remove worry, remorse, and morbid reflection that I may be of service to others. Amen.

When I retire at night...   /   /

Chronology of today's events:

Was I resentful?

    1. *Who/what*   3.   *Affects*

    2. *Cause*   4.   *My part*

Was I selfish?

Was I dishonest?

Was I afraid?

Do I owe an apology?

What have I wrongly kept secret?

Was I kind and loving toward all?

What could I have done better?

How did faith or fear rule my actions today?

Today I gave of my time ___, talent ___, treasure ___, and touch ___.

Who did I help today?

What am I grateful for today?

Who needs my prayers today?

God, forgive me where I have been resentful, selfish, dishonest, or afraid today. Help me not to keep anything to myself, but to discuss it openly with another person. Show me where I owe an apology and help me make it, and help me to be kind and loving to all people. Use me in the mainstream of life, and remove worry, remorse, and morbid reflection that I may be of service to others. Amen.

When I retire at night...   /   /

Chronology of today's events:

Was I resentful?
    1. *Who/what*   3. *Affects*

    2. *Cause*   4. *My part*

Was I selfish?

Was I dishonest?

Was I afraid?

Do I owe an apology?

What have I wrongly kept secret?

Was I kind and loving toward all?

What could I have done better?

How did faith or fear rule my actions today?

Today I gave of my time ___, talent ___, treasure ___, and touch ___.

Who did I help today?

What am I grateful for today?

Who needs my prayers today?

God, forgive me where I have been resentful, selfish, dishonest, or afraid today. Help me not to keep anything to myself, but to discuss it openly with another person. Show me where I owe an apology and help me make it, and help me to be kind and loving to all people. Use me in the mainstream of life, and remove worry, remorse, and morbid reflection that I may be of service to others. Amen.

When I retire at night... / /

Chronology of today's events:

Was I resentful?
    1. Who/what   3. Affects

    2. Cause   4. My part

Was I selfish?

Was I dishonest?

Was I afraid?

Do I owe an apology?

What have I wrongly kept secret?

Was I kind and loving toward all?

What could I have done better?

How did faith or fear rule my actions today?

Today I gave of my time ___, talent ___, treasure ___, and touch ___.

Who did I help today?

What am I grateful for today?

Who needs my prayers today?

God, forgive me where I have been resentful, selfish, dishonest, or afraid today. Help me not to keep anything to myself, but to discuss it openly with another person. Show me where I owe an apology and help me make it, and help me to be kind and loving to all people. Use me in the mainstream of life, and remove worry, remorse, and morbid reflection that I may be of service to others. Amen.

When I retire at night...   /   /

Chronology of today's events:

Was I resentful?
  1. *Who/what*   3. *Affects*
  2. *Cause*   4. *My part*

Was I selfish?

Was I dishonest?

Was I afraid?

Do I owe an apology?

What have I wrongly kept secret?

Was I kind and loving toward all?

What could I have done better?

How did faith or fear rule my actions today?

Today I gave of my time ___, talent ___, treasure ___, and touch ___.

Who did I help today?

What am I grateful for today?

Who needs my prayers today?

God, forgive me where I have been resentful, selfish, dishonest, or afraid today. Help me not to keep anything to myself, but to discuss it openly with another person. Show me where I owe an apology and help me make it, and help me to be kind and loving to all people. Use me in the mainstream of life, and remove worry, remorse, and morbid reflection that I may be of service to others. Amen.

When I retire at night...   /   /

Chronology of today's events:

Was I resentful?
    1. Who/what   3. Affects

    2. Cause   4. My part

Was I selfish?

Was I dishonest?

Was I afraid?

Do I owe an apology?

What have I wrongly kept secret?

Was I kind and loving toward all?

What could I have done better?

How did faith or fear rule my actions today?

Today I gave of my time ___, talent ___, treasure ___, and touch ___.

Who did I help today?

What am I grateful for today?

Who needs my prayers today?

God, forgive me where I have been resentful, selfish, dishonest, or afraid today. Help me not to keep anything to myself, but to discuss it openly with another person. Show me where I owe an apology and help me make it, and help me to be kind and loving to all people. Use me in the mainstream of life, and remove worry, remorse, and morbid reflection that I may be of service to others. Amen.

When I retire at night...   / /

Chronology of today's events:

Was I resentful?
 1. *Who/what*   3. *Affects*
 2. *Cause*   4. *My part*

Was I selfish?

Was I dishonest?

Was I afraid?

Do I owe an apology?

What have I wrongly kept secret?

Was I kind and loving toward all?

What could I have done better?

How did faith or fear rule my actions today?

Today I gave of my time ___, talent ___, treasure ___, and touch ___.

Who did I help today?

What am I grateful for today?

Who needs my prayers today?

God, forgive me where I have been resentful, selfish, dishonest, or afraid today. Help me not to keep anything to myself, but to discuss it openly with another person. Show me where I owe an apology and help me make it, and help me to be kind and loving to all people. Use me in the mainstream of life, and remove worry, remorse, and morbid reflection that I may be of service to others. Amen.

When I retire at night...   /   /

Chronology of today's events:

Was I resentful?
    1. *Who/what*   3. *Affects*

    2. *Cause*   4. *My part*

Was I selfish?

Was I dishonest?

Was I afraid?

Do I owe an apology?

What have I wrongly kept secret?

Was I kind and loving toward all?

What could I have done better?

How did faith or fear rule my actions today?

Today I gave of my time ___, talent ___, treasure ___, and touch ___.

Who did I help today?

What am I grateful for today?

Who needs my prayers today?

God, forgive me where I have been resentful, selfish, dishonest, or afraid today. Help me not to keep anything to myself, but to discuss it openly with another person. Show me where I owe an apology and help me make it, and help me to be kind and loving to all people. Use me in the mainstream of life, and remove worry, remorse, and morbid reflection that I may be of service to others. Amen.

When I retire at night...   /   /

Chronology of today's events:
_____
_____
_____

Was I resentful?
    1. *Who/what*　　　　　　　3. *Affects*

    2. *Cause*　　　　　　　　　4. *My part*

Was I selfish?

Was I dishonest?

Was I afraid?

Do I owe an apology?

What have I wrongly kept secret?

Was I kind and loving toward all?

What could I have done better?

How did faith or fear rule my actions today?

Today I gave of my time ___, talent ___, treasure ___, and touch ___.

Who did I help today?

What am I grateful for today?

Who needs my prayers today?

God, forgive me where I have been resentful, selfish, dishonest, or afraid today. Help me not to keep anything to myself, but to discuss it openly with another person. Show me where I owe an apology and help me make it, and help me to be kind and loving to all people. Use me in the mainstream of life, and remove worry, remorse, and morbid reflection that I may be of service to others. Amen.

When I retire at night...   /   /

Chronology of today's events:

Was I resentful?
    1. *Who/what*　　　　　　　3. *Affects*

    2. *Cause*　　　　　　　　　4. *My part*

Was I selfish?

Was I dishonest?

Was I afraid?

Do I owe an apology?

What have I wrongly kept secret?

Was I kind and loving toward all?

What could I have done better?

How did faith or fear rule my actions today?

Today I gave of my time ___, talent ___, treasure ___, and touch ___.

Who did I help today?

What am I grateful for today?

Who needs my prayers today?

God, forgive me where I have been resentful, selfish, dishonest, or afraid today. Help me not to keep anything to myself, but to discuss it openly with another person. Show me where I owe an apology and help me make it, and help me to be kind and loving to all people. Use me in the mainstream of life, and remove worry, remorse, and morbid reflection that I may be of service to others. Amen.

When I retire at night...   /   /

Chronology of today's events:

Was I resentful?
    1. *Who/what*   3. *Affects*

    2. *Cause*   4. *My part*

Was I selfish?

Was I dishonest?

Was I afraid?

Do I owe an apology?

What have I wrongly kept secret?

Was I kind and loving toward all?

What could I have done better?

How did faith or fear rule my actions today?

Today I gave of my time ___, talent ___, treasure ___, and touch ___.

Who did I help today?

What am I grateful for today?

Who needs my prayers today?

God, forgive me where I have been resentful, selfish, dishonest, or afraid today. Help me not to keep anything to myself, but to discuss it openly with another person. Show me where I owe an apology and help me make it, and help me to be kind and loving to all people. Use me in the mainstream of life, and remove worry, remorse, and morbid reflection that I may be of service to others. Amen.

When I retire at night...　　　　　　　　　　　/　　/

Chronology of today's events:

Was I resentful?
    1. Who/what　　　　　　　3. Affects

    2. Cause　　　　　　　　　4. My part

Was I selfish?

Was I dishonest?

Was I afraid?

Do I owe an apology?

What have I wrongly kept secret?

Was I kind and loving toward all?

What could I have done better?

How did faith or fear rule my actions today?

Today I gave of my time ___, talent ___, treasure ___, and touch ___.

Who did I help today?

What am I grateful for today?

Who needs my prayers today?

God, forgive me where I have been resentful, selfish, dishonest, or afraid today. Help me not to keep anything to myself, but to discuss it openly with another person. Show me where I owe an apology and help me make it, and help me to be kind and loving to all people. Use me in the mainstream of life, and remove worry, remorse, and morbid reflection that I may be of service to others. Amen.

When I retire at night...   /   /

Chronology of today's events:

_____
_____

Was I resentful?
    1. Who/what   3.   Affects

    2. Cause   4.   My part

Was I selfish?

Was I dishonest?

Was I afraid?

Do I owe an apology?

What have I wrongly kept secret?

Was I kind and loving toward all?

What could I have done better?

How did faith or fear rule my actions today?

Today I gave of my time ___, talent ___, treasure ___, and touch ___.

Who did I help today?

What am I grateful for today?

Who needs my prayers today?

God, forgive me where I have been resentful, selfish, dishonest, or afraid today. Help me not to keep anything to myself, but to discuss it openly with another person. Show me where I owe an apology and help me make it, and help me to be kind and loving to all people. Use me in the mainstream of life, and remove worry, remorse, and morbid reflection that I may be of service to others. Amen.

When I retire at night...   /   /

Chronology of today's events:

Was I resentful?
    1. Who/what　　　　　　　　*3. Affects*

    2. Cause　　　　　　　　　 *4. My part*

Was I selfish?

Was I dishonest?

Was I afraid?

Do I owe an apology?

What have I wrongly kept secret?

Was I kind and loving toward all?

What could I have done better?

How did faith or fear rule my actions today?

Today I gave of my time ___, talent ___, treasure ___, and touch ___.

Who did I help today?

What am I grateful for today?

Who needs my prayers today?

God, forgive me where I have been resentful, selfish, dishonest, or afraid today. Help me not to keep anything to myself, but to discuss it openly with another person. Show me where I owe an apology and help me make it, and help me to be kind and loving to all people. Use me in the mainstream of life, and remove worry, remorse, and morbid reflection that I may be of service to others. Amen.

When I retire at night...   /   /

Chronology of today's events:

Was I resentful?
    1. *Who/what*   3. *Affects*

    2. *Cause*   4. *My part*

Was I selfish?

Was I dishonest?

Was I afraid?

Do I owe an apology?

What have I wrongly kept secret?

Was I kind and loving toward all?

What could I have done better?

How did faith or fear rule my actions today?

Today I gave of my time ___, talent ___, treasure ___, and touch ___.

Who did I help today?

What am I grateful for today?

Who needs my prayers today?

God, forgive me where I have been resentful, selfish, dishonest, or afraid today. Help me not to keep anything to myself, but to discuss it openly with another person. Show me where I owe an apology and help me make it, and help me to be kind and loving to all people. Use me in the mainstream of life, and remove worry, remorse, and morbid reflection that I may be of service to others. Amen.

When I retire at night...   /   /

Chronology of today's events:

Was I resentful?
    1. *Who/what*   3. *Affects*

    2. *Cause*   4. *My part*

Was I selfish?

Was I dishonest?

Was I afraid?

Do I owe an apology?

What have I wrongly kept secret?

Was I kind and loving toward all?

What could I have done better?

How did faith or fear rule my actions today?

Today I gave of my time ___, talent ___, treasure ___, and touch ___.

Who did I help today?

What am I grateful for today?

Who needs my prayers today?

God, forgive me where I have been resentful, selfish, dishonest, or afraid today. Help me not to keep anything to myself, but to discuss it openly with another person. Show me where I owe an apology and help me make it, and help me to be kind and loving to all people. Use me in the mainstream of life, and remove worry, remorse, and morbid reflection that I may be of service to others. Amen.

When I retire at night...   /   /

Chronology of today's events:

Was I resentful?
    1. *Who/what*　　　　　3. *Affects*

    2. *Cause*　　　　　　　4. *My part*

Was I selfish?

Was I dishonest?

Was I afraid?

Do I owe an apology?

What have I wrongly kept secret?

Was I kind and loving toward all?

What could I have done better?

How did faith or fear rule my actions today?

Today I gave of my time ___, talent ___, treasure ___, and touch ___.

Who did I help today?

What am I grateful for today?

Who needs my prayers today?

God, forgive me where I have been resentful, selfish, dishonest, or afraid today. Help me not to keep anything to myself, but to discuss it openly with another person. Show me where I owe an apology and help me make it, and help me to be kind and loving to all people. Use me in the mainstream of life, and remove worry, remorse, and morbid reflection that I may be of service to others. Amen.

When I retire at night...   /   /

Chronology of today's events:

Was I resentful?
    1. *Who/what*   3. *Affects*

    2. *Cause*   4. *My part*

Was I selfish?

Was I dishonest?

Was I afraid?

Do I owe an apology?

What have I wrongly kept secret?

Was I kind and loving toward all?

What could I have done better?

How did faith or fear rule my actions today?

Today I gave of my time ___, talent ___, treasure ___, and touch ___.

Who did I help today?

What am I grateful for today?

Who needs my prayers today?

God, forgive me where I have been resentful, selfish, dishonest, or afraid today. Help me not to keep anything to myself, but to discuss it openly with another person. Show me where I owe an apology and help me make it, and help me to be kind and loving to all people. Use me in the mainstream of life, and remove worry, remorse, and morbid reflection that I may be of service to others. Amen.

When I retire at night...   /   /

Chronology of today's events:

Was I resentful?
1. Who/what
2. Cause
3. Affects
4. My part

Was I selfish?

Was I dishonest?

Was I afraid?

Do I owe an apology?

What have I wrongly kept secret?

Was I kind and loving toward all?

What could I have done better?

How did faith or fear rule my actions today?

Today I gave of my time ___, talent ___, treasure ___, and touch ___.

Who did I help today?

What am I grateful for today?

Who needs my prayers today?

God, forgive me where I have been resentful, selfish, dishonest, or afraid today. Help me not to keep anything to myself, but to discuss it openly with another person. Show me where I owe an apology and help me make it, and help me to be kind and loving to all people. Use me in the mainstream of life, and remove worry, remorse, and morbid reflection that I may be of service to others. Amen.

When I retire at night...   /   /

Chronology of today's events:

Was I resentful?
    1. Who/what   *3. Affects*

    2. Cause   *4. My part*

Was I selfish?

Was I dishonest?

Was I afraid?

Do I owe an apology?

What have I wrongly kept secret?

Was I kind and loving toward all?

What could I have done better?

How did faith or fear rule my actions today?

Today I gave of my time ___, talent ___, treasure ___, and touch ___.

Who did I help today?

What am I grateful for today?

Who needs my prayers today?

God, forgive me where I have been resentful, selfish, dishonest, or afraid today. Help me not to keep anything to myself, but to discuss it openly with another person. Show me where I owe an apology and help me make it, and help me to be kind and loving to all people. Use me in the mainstream of life, and remove worry, remorse, and morbid reflection that I may be of service to others. Amen.

When I retire at night...   /   /

Chronology of today's events:

Was I resentful?
    1. *Who/what*   3. *Affects*

    2. *Cause*   4. *My part*

Was I selfish?

Was I dishonest?

Was I afraid?

Do I owe an apology?

What have I wrongly kept secret?

Was I kind and loving toward all?

What could I have done better?

How did faith or fear rule my actions today?

Today I gave of my time ___, talent ___, treasure ___, and touch ___.

Who did I help today?

What am I grateful for today?

Who needs my prayers today?

God, forgive me where I have been resentful, selfish, dishonest, or afraid today. Help me not to keep anything to myself, but to discuss it openly with another person. Show me where I owe an apology and help me make it, and help me to be kind and loving to all people. Use me in the mainstream of life, and remove worry, remorse, and morbid reflection that I may be of service to others. Amen.

When I retire at night...   /   /

Chronology of today's events:

Was I resentful?
    1. Who/what   3.   Affects

    2. Cause   4.   My part

Was I selfish?

Was I dishonest?

Was I afraid?

Do I owe an apology?

What have I wrongly kept secret?

Was I kind and loving toward all?

What could I have done better?

How did faith or fear rule my actions today?

Today I gave of my time ____, talent ____, treasure ____, and touch ____.

Who did I help today?

What am I grateful for today?

Who needs my prayers today?

God, forgive me where I have been resentful, selfish, dishonest, or afraid today. Help me not to keep anything to myself, but to discuss it openly with another person. Show me where I owe an apology and help me make it, and help me to be kind and loving to all people. Use me in the mainstream of life, and remove worry, remorse, and morbid reflection that I may be of service to others. Amen.

When I retire at night...   /   /

Chronology of today's events:

Was I resentful?
    1. *Who/what*   3. *Affects*

    2. *Cause*   4. *My part*

Was I selfish?

Was I dishonest?

Was I afraid?

Do I owe an apology?

What have I wrongly kept secret?

Was I kind and loving toward all?

What could I have done better?

How did faith or fear rule my actions today?

Today I gave of my time ___, talent ___, treasure ___, and touch ___.

Who did I help today?

What am I grateful for today?

Who needs my prayers today?

God, forgive me where I have been resentful, selfish, dishonest, or afraid today. Help me not to keep anything to myself, but to discuss it openly with another person. Show me where I owe an apology and help me make it, and help me to be kind and loving to all people. Use me in the mainstream of life, and remove worry, remorse, and morbid reflection that I may be of service to others. Amen.

When I retire at night...   /   /

Chronology of today's events:

Was I resentful?
    1. Who/what   3. Affects

    2. Cause   4. My part

Was I selfish?

Was I dishonest?

Was I afraid?

Do I owe an apology?

What have I wrongly kept secret?

Was I kind and loving toward all?

What could I have done better?

How did faith or fear rule my actions today?

Today I gave of my time ___, talent ___, treasure ___, and touch ___.

Who did I help today?

What am I grateful for today?

Who needs my prayers today?

God, forgive me where I have been resentful, selfish, dishonest, or afraid today. Help me not to keep anything to myself, but to discuss it openly with another person. Show me where I owe an apology and help me make it, and help me to be kind and loving to all people. Use me in the mainstream of life, and remove worry, remorse, and morbid reflection that I may be of service to others. Amen.

When I retire at night...   /   /

Chronology of today's events:

Was I resentful?
    1. Who/what   *3.   Affects*

    2. Cause   *4.   My part*

Was I selfish?

Was I dishonest?

Was I afraid?

Do I owe an apology?

What have I wrongly kept secret?

Was I kind and loving toward all?

What could I have done better?

How did faith or fear rule my actions today?

Today I gave of my time ___, talent ___, treasure ___, and touch ___.

Who did I help today?

What am I grateful for today?

Who needs my prayers today?

God, forgive me where I have been resentful, selfish, dishonest, or afraid today. Help me not to keep anything to myself, but to discuss it openly with another person. Show me where I owe an apology and help me make it, and help me to be kind and loving to all people. Use me in the mainstream of life, and remove worry, remorse, and morbid reflection that I may be of service to others. Amen.

When I retire at night...   /   /

Chronology of today's events:

Was I resentful?
    1. Who/what   *3. Affects*

    2. Cause   *4. My part*

Was I selfish?

Was I dishonest?

Was I afraid?

Do I owe an apology?

What have I wrongly kept secret?

Was I kind and loving toward all?

What could I have done better?

How did faith or fear rule my actions today?

Today I gave of my time ___, talent ___, treasure ___, and touch ___.

Who did I help today?

What am I grateful for today?

Who needs my prayers today?

God, forgive me where I have been resentful, selfish, dishonest, or afraid today. Help me not to keep anything to myself, but to discuss it openly with another person. Show me where I owe an apology and help me make it, and help me to be kind and loving to all people. Use me in the mainstream of life, and remove worry, remorse, and morbid reflection that I may be of service to others. Amen.

When I retire at night...					/ /

Chronology of today's events:

Was I resentful?
    1. *Who/what*   3. *Affects*

    2. *Cause*   4. *My part*

Was I selfish?

Was I dishonest?

Was I afraid?

Do I owe an apology?

What have I wrongly kept secret?

Was I kind and loving toward all?

What could I have done better?

How did faith or fear rule my actions today?

Today I gave of my time ___, talent ___, treasure ___, and touch ___.

Who did I help today?

What am I grateful for today?

Who needs my prayers today?

God, forgive me where I have been resentful, selfish, dishonest, or afraid today. Help me not to keep anything to myself, but to discuss it openly with another person. Show me where I owe an apology and help me make it, and help me to be kind and loving to all people. Use me in the mainstream of life, and remove worry, remorse, and morbid reflection that I may be of service to others. Amen.

When I retire at night...   /   /

Chronology of today's events:

Was I resentful?
    1. *Who/what*   3. *Affects*

    2. *Cause*   4. *My part*

Was I selfish?

Was I dishonest?

Was I afraid?

Do I owe an apology?

What have I wrongly kept secret?

Was I kind and loving toward all?

What could I have done better?

How did faith or fear rule my actions today?

Today I gave of my time ___, talent ___, treasure ___, and touch ___.

Who did I help today?

What am I grateful for today?

Who needs my prayers today?

God, forgive me where I have been resentful, selfish, dishonest, or afraid today. Help me not to keep anything to myself, but to discuss it openly with another person. Show me where I owe an apology and help me make it, and help me to be kind and loving to all people. Use me in the mainstream of life, and remove worry, remorse, and morbid reflection that I may be of service to others. Amen.

When I retire at night...   /   /

Chronology of today's events:

Was I resentful?
    1. *Who/what*   3. *Affects*

    2. *Cause*   4. *My part*

Was I selfish?

Was I dishonest?

Was I afraid?

Do I owe an apology?

What have I wrongly kept secret?

Was I kind and loving toward all?

What could I have done better?

How did faith or fear rule my actions today?

Today I gave of my time ___, talent ___, treasure ___, and touch ___.

Who did I help today?

What am I grateful for today?

Who needs my prayers today?

God, forgive me where I have been resentful, selfish, dishonest, or afraid today. Help me not to keep anything to myself, but to discuss it openly with another person. Show me where I owe an apology and help me make it, and help me to be kind and loving to all people. Use me in the mainstream of life, and remove worry, remorse, and morbid reflection that I may be of service to others. Amen.

When I retire at night...   /   /

Chronology of today's events:

Was I resentful?
    1. Who/what
    2. Cause
    3. Affects
    4. My part

Was I selfish?

Was I dishonest?

Was I afraid?

Do I owe an apology?

What have I wrongly kept secret?

Was I kind and loving toward all?

What could I have done better?

How did faith or fear rule my actions today?

Today I gave of my time ___, talent ___, treasure ___, and touch ___.

Who did I help today?

What am I grateful for today?

Who needs my prayers today?

God, forgive me where I have been resentful, selfish, dishonest, or afraid today. Help me not to keep anything to myself, but to discuss it openly with another person. Show me where I owe an apology and help me make it, and help me to be kind and loving to all people. Use me in the mainstream of life, and remove worry, remorse, and morbid reflection that I may be of service to others. Amen.

When I retire at night...   /   /

Chronology of today's events:

Was I resentful?
    1. Who/what   3. Affects

    2. Cause   4. My part

Was I selfish?

Was I dishonest?

Was I afraid?

Do I owe an apology?

What have I wrongly kept secret?

Was I kind and loving toward all?

What could I have done better?

How did faith or fear rule my actions today?

Today I gave of my time ___, talent ___, treasure ___, and touch ___.

Who did I help today?

What am I grateful for today?

Who needs my prayers today?

God, forgive me where I have been resentful, selfish, dishonest, or afraid today. Help me not to keep anything to myself, but to discuss it openly with another person. Show me where I owe an apology and help me make it, and help me to be kind and loving to all people. Use me in the mainstream of life, and remove worry, remorse, and morbid reflection that I may be of service to others. Amen.

When I retire at night...   /   /

Chronology of today's events:

Was I resentful?
    1. *Who/what*   3. *Affects*

    2. *Cause*   4. *My part*

Was I selfish?

Was I dishonest?

Was I afraid?

Do I owe an apology?

What have I wrongly kept secret?

Was I kind and loving toward all?

What could I have done better?

How did faith or fear rule my actions today?

Today I gave of my time ___, talent ___, treasure ___, and touch ___.

Who did I help today?

What am I grateful for today?

Who needs my prayers today?

God, forgive me where I have been resentful, selfish, dishonest, or afraid today. Help me not to keep anything to myself, but to discuss it openly with another person. Show me where I owe an apology and help me make it, and help me to be kind and loving to all people. Use me in the mainstream of life, and remove worry, remorse, and morbid reflection that I may be of service to others. Amen.

When I retire at night...   /   /

Chronology of today's events:

Was I resentful?
    1. *Who/what*   3.   *Affects*

    2. *Cause*   4.   *My part*

Was I selfish?

Was I dishonest?

Was I afraid?

Do I owe an apology?

What have I wrongly kept secret?

Was I kind and loving toward all?

What could I have done better?

How did faith or fear rule my actions today?

Today I gave of my time ___, talent ___, treasure ___, and touch ___.

Who did I help today?

What am I grateful for today?

Who needs my prayers today?

God, forgive me where I have been resentful, selfish, dishonest, or afraid today. Help me not to keep anything to myself, but to discuss it openly with another person. Show me where I owe an apology and help me make it, and help me to be kind and loving to all people. Use me in the mainstream of life, and remove worry, remorse, and morbid reflection that I may be of service to others. Amen.

When I retire at night...   /   /

Chronology of today's events:

Was I resentful?
    1. *Who/what*   3. *Affects*

    2. *Cause*   4. *My part*

Was I selfish?

Was I dishonest?

Was I afraid?

Do I owe an apology?

What have I wrongly kept secret?

Was I kind and loving toward all?

What could I have done better?

How did faith or fear rule my actions today?

Today I gave of my time ___, talent ___, treasure ___, and touch ___.

Who did I help today?

What am I grateful for today?

Who needs my prayers today?

God, forgive me where I have been resentful, selfish, dishonest, or afraid today. Help me not to keep anything to myself, but to discuss it openly with another person. Show me where I owe an apology and help me make it, and help me to be kind and loving to all people. Use me in the mainstream of life, and remove worry, remorse, and morbid reflection that I may be of service to others. Amen.

When I retire at night...   /   /

Chronology of today's events:

Was I resentful?
    1. *Who/what*　　　　　　　3. *Affects*

    2. *Cause*　　　　　　　　　4. *My part*

Was I selfish?

Was I dishonest?

Was I afraid?

Do I owe an apology?

What have I wrongly kept secret?

Was I kind and loving toward all?

What could I have done better?

How did faith or fear rule my actions today?

Today I gave of my time ___, talent ___, treasure ___, and touch ___.

Who did I help today?

What am I grateful for today?

Who needs my prayers today?

God, forgive me where I have been resentful, selfish, dishonest, or afraid today. Help me not to keep anything to myself, but to discuss it openly with another person. Show me where I owe an apology and help me make it, and help me to be kind and loving to all people. Use me in the mainstream of life, and remove worry, remorse, and morbid reflection that I may be of service to others. Amen.

When I retire at night...   /   /

Chronology of today's events:

Was I resentful?
    1. Who/what   3.   Affects

    2. Cause   4.   My part

Was I selfish?

Was I dishonest?

Was I afraid?

Do I owe an apology?

What have I wrongly kept secret?

Was I kind and loving toward all?

What could I have done better?

How did faith or fear rule my actions today?

Today I gave of my time ___, talent ___, treasure ___, and touch ___.

Who did I help today?

What am I grateful for today?

Who needs my prayers today?

God, forgive me where I have been resentful, selfish, dishonest, or afraid today. Help me not to keep anything to myself, but to discuss it openly with another person. Show me where I owe an apology and help me make it, and help me to be kind and loving to all people. Use me in the mainstream of life, and remove worry, remorse, and morbid reflection that I may be of service to others. Amen.

When I retire at night...   /   /

Chronology of today's events:

Was I resentful?
    1. *Who/what*   3. *Affects*

    2. *Cause*   4. *My part*

Was I selfish?

Was I dishonest?

Was I afraid?

Do I owe an apology?

What have I wrongly kept secret?

Was I kind and loving toward all?

What could I have done better?

How did faith or fear rule my actions today?

Today I gave of my time ___, talent ___, treasure ___, and touch ___.

Who did I help today?

What am I grateful for today?

Who needs my prayers today?

God, forgive me where I have been resentful, selfish, dishonest, or afraid today. Help me not to keep anything to myself, but to discuss it openly with another person. Show me where I owe an apology and help me make it, and help me to be kind and loving to all people. Use me in the mainstream of life, and remove worry, remorse, and morbid reflection that I may be of service to others. Amen.

When I retire at night...   /   /

Chronology of today's events:

Was I resentful?
    1. Who/what
    2. Cause
    3. Affects
    4. My part

Was I selfish?

Was I dishonest?

Was I afraid?

Do I owe an apology?

What have I wrongly kept secret?

Was I kind and loving toward all?

What could I have done better?

How did faith or fear rule my actions today?

Today I gave of my time ___, talent ___, treasure ___, and touch ___.

Who did I help today?

What am I grateful for today?

Who needs my prayers today?

God, forgive me where I have been resentful, selfish, dishonest, or afraid today. Help me not to keep anything to myself, but to discuss it openly with another person. Show me where I owe an apology and help me make it, and help me to be kind and loving to all people. Use me in the mainstream of life, and remove worry, remorse, and morbid reflection that I may be of service to others. Amen.

When I retire at night...   /   /

Chronology of today's events:

Was I resentful?
    1. *Who/what*　　　　　　　　3. *Affects*

    2. *Cause*　　　　　　　　　　4. *My part*

Was I selfish?

Was I dishonest?

Was I afraid?

Do I owe an apology?

What have I wrongly kept secret?

Was I kind and loving toward all?

What could I have done better?

How did faith or fear rule my actions today?

Today I gave of my time ___, talent ___, treasure ___, and touch ___.

Who did I help today?

What am I grateful for today?

Who needs my prayers today?

God, forgive me where I have been resentful, selfish, dishonest, or afraid today. Help me not to keep anything to myself, but to discuss it openly with another person. Show me where I owe an apology and help me make it, and help me to be kind and loving to all people. Use me in the mainstream of life, and remove worry, remorse, and morbid reflection that I may be of service to others. Amen.

When I retire at night...   /   /

Chronology of today's events:

Was I resentful?
    1. *Who/what*   3. *Affects*

    2. *Cause*   4. *My part*

Was I selfish?

Was I dishonest?

Was I afraid?

Do I owe an apology?

What have I wrongly kept secret?

Was I kind and loving toward all?

What could I have done better?

How did faith or fear rule my actions today?

Today I gave of my time ___, talent ___, treasure ___, and touch ___.

Who did I help today?

What am I grateful for today?

Who needs my prayers today?

God, forgive me where I have been resentful, selfish, dishonest, or afraid today. Help me not to keep anything to myself, but to discuss it openly with another person. Show me where I owe an apology and help me make it, and help me to be kind and loving to all people. Use me in the mainstream of life, and remove worry, remorse, and morbid reflection that I may be of service to others. Amen.

When I retire at night...   /   /

Chronology of today's events:

Was I resentful?
    1. *Who/what*   3. *Affects*

    2. *Cause*   4. *My part*

Was I selfish?

Was I dishonest?

Was I afraid?

Do I owe an apology?

What have I wrongly kept secret?

Was I kind and loving toward all?

What could I have done better?

How did faith or fear rule my actions today?

Today I gave of my time ___, talent ___, treasure ___, and touch ___.

Who did I help today?

What am I grateful for today?

Who needs my prayers today?

God, forgive me where I have been resentful, selfish, dishonest, or afraid today. Help me not to keep anything to myself, but to discuss it openly with another person. Show me where I owe an apology and help me make it, and help me to be kind and loving to all people. Use me in the mainstream of life, and remove worry, remorse, and morbid reflection that I may be of service to others. Amen.

When I retire at night...   /   /

Chronology of today's events:

Was I resentful?
    1. *Who/what*   3.   *Affects*

    2. *Cause*   4.   *My part*

Was I selfish?

Was I dishonest?

Was I afraid?

Do I owe an apology?

What have I wrongly kept secret?

Was I kind and loving toward all?

What could I have done better?

How did faith or fear rule my actions today?

Today I gave of my time ___, talent ___, treasure ___, and touch ___.

Who did I help today?

What am I grateful for today?

Who needs my prayers today?

God, forgive me where I have been resentful, selfish, dishonest, or afraid today. Help me not to keep anything to myself, but to discuss it openly with another person. Show me where I owe an apology and help me make it, and help me to be kind and loving to all people. Use me in the mainstream of life, and remove worry, remorse, and morbid reflection that I may be of service to others. Amen.

When I retire at night...   /   /

Chronology of today's events:

Was I resentful?
    1. Who/what
    2. Cause
    3. Affects
    4. My part

Was I selfish?

Was I dishonest?

Was I afraid?

Do I owe an apology?

What have I wrongly kept secret?

Was I kind and loving toward all?

What could I have done better?

How did faith or fear rule my actions today?

Today I gave of my time ___, talent ___, treasure ___, and touch ___.

Who did I help today?

What am I grateful for today?

Who needs my prayers today?

God, forgive me where I have been resentful, selfish, dishonest, or afraid today. Help me not to keep anything to myself, but to discuss it openly with another person. Show me where I owe an apology and help me make it, and help me to be kind and loving to all people. Use me in the mainstream of life, and remove worry, remorse, and morbid reflection that I may be of service to others. Amen.

When I retire at night...   /   /

Chronology of today's events:

Was I resentful?
    1. *Who/what*   3. *Affects*

    2. *Cause*   4. *My part*

Was I selfish?

Was I dishonest?

Was I afraid?

Do I owe an apology?

What have I wrongly kept secret?

Was I kind and loving toward all?

What could I have done better?

How did faith or fear rule my actions today?

Today I gave of my time ___, talent ___, treasure ___, and touch ___.

Who did I help today?

What am I grateful for today?

Who needs my prayers today?

God, forgive me where I have been resentful, selfish, dishonest, or afraid today. Help me not to keep anything to myself, but to discuss it openly with another person. Show me where I owe an apology and help me make it, and help me to be kind and loving to all people. Use me in the mainstream of life, and remove worry, remorse, and morbid reflection that I may be of service to others. Amen.

When I retire at night...   /   /

Chronology of today's events:

Was I resentful?
    1. *Who/what*　　　　　　　3. *Affects*

    2. *Cause*　　　　　　　　　4. *My part*

Was I selfish?

Was I dishonest?

Was I afraid?

Do I owe an apology?

What have I wrongly kept secret?

Was I kind and loving toward all?

What could I have done better?

How did faith or fear rule my actions today?

Today I gave of my time ___, talent ___, treasure ___, and touch ___.

Who did I help today?

What am I grateful for today?

Who needs my prayers today?

God, forgive me where I have been resentful, selfish, dishonest, or afraid today. Help me not to keep anything to myself, but to discuss it openly with another person. Show me where I owe an apology and help me make it, and help me to be kind and loving to all people. Use me in the mainstream of life, and remove worry, remorse, and morbid reflection that I may be of service to others. Amen.

When I retire at night...   /   /

Chronology of today's events:

Was I resentful?
    1. Who/what   3. Affects

    2. Cause   4. My part

Was I selfish?

Was I dishonest?

Was I afraid?

Do I owe an apology?

What have I wrongly kept secret?

Was I kind and loving toward all?

What could I have done better?

How did faith or fear rule my actions today?

Today I gave of my time ___, talent ___, treasure ___, and touch ___.

Who did I help today?

What am I grateful for today?

Who needs my prayers today?

God, forgive me where I have been resentful, selfish, dishonest, or afraid today. Help me not to keep anything to myself, but to discuss it openly with another person. Show me where I owe an apology and help me make it, and help me to be kind and loving to all people. Use me in the mainstream of life, and remove worry, remorse, and morbid reflection that I may be of service to others. Amen.

When I retire at night...   /   /

Chronology of today's events:

Was I resentful?
    1. *Who/what*   3. *Affects*

    2. *Cause*   4. *My part*

Was I selfish?

Was I dishonest?

Was I afraid?

Do I owe an apology?

What have I wrongly kept secret?

Was I kind and loving toward all?

What could I have done better?

How did faith or fear rule my actions today?

Today I gave of my time ___, talent ___, treasure ___, and touch ___.

Who did I help today?

What am I grateful for today?

Who needs my prayers today?

God, forgive me where I have been resentful, selfish, dishonest, or afraid today. Help me not to keep anything to myself, but to discuss it openly with another person. Show me where I owe an apology and help me make it, and help me to be kind and loving to all people. Use me in the mainstream of life, and remove worry, remorse, and morbid reflection that I may be of service to others. Amen.

When I retire at night...   /   /

Chronology of today's events:

Was I resentful?
    1. Who/what   3. Affects

    2. Cause   4. My part

Was I selfish?

Was I dishonest?

Was I afraid?

Do I owe an apology?

What have I wrongly kept secret?

Was I kind and loving toward all?

What could I have done better?

How did faith or fear rule my actions today?

Today I gave of my time ___, talent ___, treasure ___, and touch ___.

Who did I help today?

What am I grateful for today?

Who needs my prayers today?

God, forgive me where I have been resentful, selfish, dishonest, or afraid today. Help me not to keep anything to myself, but to discuss it openly with another person. Show me where I owe an apology and help me make it, and help me to be kind and loving to all people. Use me in the mainstream of life, and remove worry, remorse, and morbid reflection that I may be of service to others. Amen.

When I retire at night...   /   /

Chronology of today's events:

Was I resentful?
    1. *Who/what*   3. *Affects*

    2. *Cause*   4. *My part*

Was I selfish?

Was I dishonest?

Was I afraid?

Do I owe an apology?

What have I wrongly kept secret?

Was I kind and loving toward all?

What could I have done better?

How did faith or fear rule my actions today?

Today I gave of my time ____, talent ____, treasure ____, and touch ____.

Who did I help today?

What am I grateful for today?

Who needs my prayers today?

God, forgive me where I have been resentful, selfish, dishonest, or afraid today. Help me not to keep anything to myself, but to discuss it openly with another person. Show me where I owe an apology and help me make it, and help me to be kind and loving to all people. Use me in the mainstream of life, and remove worry, remorse, and morbid reflection that I may be of service to others. Amen.

When I retire at night...   /   /

Chronology of today's events:

Was I resentful?
    1. *Who/what*   3.   *Affects*

    2. *Cause*   4.   *My part*

Was I selfish?

Was I dishonest?

Was I afraid?

Do I owe an apology?

What have I wrongly kept secret?

Was I kind and loving toward all?

What could I have done better?

How did faith or fear rule my actions today?

Today I gave of my time ___, talent ___, treasure ___, and touch ___.

Who did I help today?

What am I grateful for today?

Who needs my prayers today?

God, forgive me where I have been resentful, selfish, dishonest, or afraid today. Help me not to keep anything to myself, but to discuss it openly with another person. Show me where I owe an apology and help me make it, and help me to be kind and loving to all people. Use me in the mainstream of life, and remove worry, remorse, and morbid reflection that I may be of service to others. Amen.

When I retire at night...   /   /

Chronology of today's events:

Was I resentful?
    1. *Who/what*   3. *Affects*

    2. *Cause*   4. *My part*

Was I selfish?

Was I dishonest?

Was I afraid?

Do I owe an apology?

What have I wrongly kept secret?

Was I kind and loving toward all?

What could I have done better?

How did faith or fear rule my actions today?

Today I gave of my time ___, talent ___, treasure ___, and touch ___.

Who did I help today?

What am I grateful for today?

Who needs my prayers today?

God, forgive me where I have been resentful, selfish, dishonest, or afraid today. Help me not to keep anything to myself, but to discuss it openly with another person. Show me where I owe an apology and help me make it, and help me to be kind and loving to all people. Use me in the mainstream of life, and remove worry, remorse, and morbid reflection that I may be of service to others. Amen.

When I retire at night...   /   /

Chronology of today's events:

Was I resentful?
    1. *Who/what*   3. *Affects*

    2. *Cause*   4. *My part*

Was I selfish?

Was I dishonest?

Was I afraid?

Do I owe an apology?

What have I wrongly kept secret?

Was I kind and loving toward all?

What could I have done better?

How did faith or fear rule my actions today?

Today I gave of my time ___, talent ___, treasure ___, and touch ___.

Who did I help today?

What am I grateful for today?

Who needs my prayers today?

God, forgive me where I have been resentful, selfish, dishonest, or afraid today. Help me not to keep anything to myself, but to discuss it openly with another person. Show me where I owe an apology and help me make it, and help me to be kind and loving to all people. Use me in the mainstream of life, and remove worry, remorse, and morbid reflection that I may be of service to others. Amen.

When I retire at night...   /   /

Chronology of today's events:

Was I resentful?
    1. *Who/what*   3. *Affects*

    2. *Cause*   4. *My part*

Was I selfish?

Was I dishonest?

Was I afraid?

Do I owe an apology?

What have I wrongly kept secret?

Was I kind and loving toward all?

What could I have done better?

How did faith or fear rule my actions today?

Today I gave of my time ___, talent ___, treasure ___, and touch ___.

Who did I help today?

What am I grateful for today?

Who needs my prayers today?

God, forgive me where I have been resentful, selfish, dishonest, or afraid today. Help me not to keep anything to myself, but to discuss it openly with another person. Show me where I owe an apology and help me make it, and help me to be kind and loving to all people. Use me in the mainstream of life, and remove worry, remorse, and morbid reflection that I may be of service to others. Amen.

When I retire at night...   /   /

Chronology of today's events:

Was I resentful?
    1. Who/what   3.   Affects

    2. Cause   4.   My part

Was I selfish?

Was I dishonest?

Was I afraid?

Do I owe an apology?

What have I wrongly kept secret?

Was I kind and loving toward all?

What could I have done better?

How did faith or fear rule my actions today?

Today I gave of my time ___, talent ___, treasure ___, and touch ___.

Who did I help today?

What am I grateful for today?

Who needs my prayers today?

God, forgive me where I have been resentful, selfish, dishonest, or afraid today. Help me not to keep anything to myself, but to discuss it openly with another person. Show me where I owe an apology and help me make it, and help me to be kind and loving to all people. Use me in the mainstream of life, and remove worry, remorse, and morbid reflection that I may be of service to others. Amen.

When I retire at night...   /   /

Chronology of today's events:

Was I resentful?
    1. *Who/what*   3. *Affects*

    2. *Cause*   4. *My part*

Was I selfish?

Was I dishonest?

Was I afraid?

Do I owe an apology?

What have I wrongly kept secret?

Was I kind and loving toward all?

What could I have done better?

How did faith or fear rule my actions today?

Today I gave of my time ___, talent ___, treasure ___, and touch ___.

Who did I help today?

What am I grateful for today?

Who needs my prayers today?

God, forgive me where I have been resentful, selfish, dishonest, or afraid today. Help me not to keep anything to myself, but to discuss it openly with another person. Show me where I owe an apology and help me make it, and help me to be kind and loving to all people. Use me in the mainstream of life, and remove worry, remorse, and morbid reflection that I may be of service to others. Amen.

When I retire at night...   /   /

Chronology of today's events:

Was I resentful?
   1. *Who/what*   3. *Affects*

   2. *Cause*   4. *My part*

Was I selfish?

Was I dishonest?

Was I afraid?

Do I owe an apology?

What have I wrongly kept secret?

Was I kind and loving toward all?

What could I have done better?

How did faith or fear rule my actions today?

Today I gave of my time ___, talent ___, treasure ___, and touch ___.

Who did I help today?

What am I grateful for today?

Who needs my prayers today?

God, forgive me where I have been resentful, selfish, dishonest, or afraid today. Help me not to keep anything to myself, but to discuss it openly with another person. Show me where I owe an apology and help me make it, and help me to be kind and loving to all people. Use me in the mainstream of life, and remove worry, remorse, and morbid reflection that I may be of service to others. Amen.

When I retire at night...   /   /

Chronology of today's events:

Was I resentful?

    1. *Who/what*   3. *Affects*

    2. *Cause*   4. *My part*

Was I selfish?

Was I dishonest?

Was I afraid?

Do I owe an apology?

What have I wrongly kept secret?

Was I kind and loving toward all?

What could I have done better?

How did faith or fear rule my actions today?

Today I gave of my time ___, talent ___, treasure ___, and touch ___.

Who did I help today?

What am I grateful for today?

Who needs my prayers today?

God, forgive me where I have been resentful, selfish, dishonest, or afraid today. Help me not to keep anything to myself, but to discuss it openly with another person. Show me where I owe an apology and help me make it, and help me to be kind and loving to all people. Use me in the mainstream of life, and remove worry, remorse, and morbid reflection that I may be of service to others. Amen.

When I retire at night…   /   /

Chronology of today's events:

Was I resentful?
    1. Who/what   3.   Affects

    2. Cause   4.   My part

Was I selfish?

Was I dishonest?

Was I afraid?

Do I owe an apology?

What have I wrongly kept secret?

Was I kind and loving toward all?

What could I have done better?

How did faith or fear rule my actions today?

Today I gave of my time ___, talent ___, treasure ___, and touch ___.

Who did I help today?

What am I grateful for today?

Who needs my prayers today?

God, forgive me where I have been resentful, selfish, dishonest, or afraid today. Help me not to keep anything to myself, but to discuss it openly with another person. Show me where I owe an apology and help me make it, and help me to be kind and loving to all people. Use me in the mainstream of life, and remove worry, remorse, and morbid reflection that I may be of service to others. Amen.

When I retire at night...   /   /

Chronology of today's events:

Was I resentful?
    1. *Who/what*   3. *Affects*

    2. *Cause*   4. *My part*

Was I selfish?

Was I dishonest?

Was I afraid?

Do I owe an apology?

What have I wrongly kept secret?

Was I kind and loving toward all?

What could I have done better?

How did faith or fear rule my actions today?

Today I gave of my time ___, talent ___, treasure ___, and touch ___.

Who did I help today?

What am I grateful for today?

Who needs my prayers today?

God, forgive me where I have been resentful, selfish, dishonest, or afraid today. Help me not to keep anything to myself, but to discuss it openly with another person. Show me where I owe an apology and help me make it, and help me to be kind and loving to all people. Use me in the mainstream of life, and remove worry, remorse, and morbid reflection that I may be of service to others. Amen.

When I retire at night...   /   /

Chronology of today's events:

Was I resentful?
    1. *Who/what*   3.   *Affects*

    2. *Cause*   4.   *My part*

Was I selfish?

Was I dishonest?

Was I afraid?

Do I owe an apology?

What have I wrongly kept secret?

Was I kind and loving toward all?

What could I have done better?

How did faith or fear rule my actions today?

Today I gave of my time ___, talent ___, treasure ___, and touch ___.

Who did I help today?

What am I grateful for today?

Who needs my prayers today?

God, forgive me where I have been resentful, selfish, dishonest, or afraid today. Help me not to keep anything to myself, but to discuss it openly with another person. Show me where I owe an apology and help me make it, and help me to be kind and loving to all people. Use me in the mainstream of life, and remove worry, remorse, and morbid reflection that I may be of service to others. Amen.

When I retire at night…   /   /

Chronology of today's events:

Was I resentful?
    1. *Who/what*   3. *Affects*

    2. *Cause*   4. *My part*

Was I selfish?

Was I dishonest?

Was I afraid?

Do I owe an apology?

What have I wrongly kept secret?

Was I kind and loving toward all?

What could I have done better?

How did faith or fear rule my actions today?

Today I gave of my time ___, talent ___, treasure ___, and touch ___.

Who did I help today?

What am I grateful for today?

Who needs my prayers today?

God, forgive me where I have been resentful, selfish, dishonest, or afraid today. Help me not to keep anything to myself, but to discuss it openly with another person. Show me where I owe an apology and help me make it, and help me to be kind and loving to all people. Use me in the mainstream of life, and remove worry, remorse, and morbid reflection that I may be of service to others. Amen.

When I retire at night...   /   /

Chronology of today's events:

Was I resentful?
    1. *Who/what*   3. *Affects*

    2. *Cause*   4. *My part*

Was I selfish?

Was I dishonest?

Was I afraid?

Do I owe an apology?

What have I wrongly kept secret?

Was I kind and loving toward all?

What could I have done better?

How did faith or fear rule my actions today?

Today I gave of my time ___, talent ___, treasure ___, and touch ___.

Who did I help today?

What am I grateful for today?

Who needs my prayers today?

God, forgive me where I have been resentful, selfish, dishonest, or afraid today. Help me not to keep anything to myself, but to discuss it openly with another person. Show me where I owe an apology and help me make it, and help me to be kind and loving to all people. Use me in the mainstream of life, and remove worry, remorse, and morbid reflection that I may be of service to others. Amen.

When I retire at night...   /   /

Chronology of today's events:

Was I resentful?
    1. *Who/what*　　　　　　　3. *Affects*

    2. *Cause*　　　　　　　　　4. *My part*

Was I selfish?

Was I dishonest?

Was I afraid?

Do I owe an apology?

What have I wrongly kept secret?

Was I kind and loving toward all?

What could I have done better?

How did faith or fear rule my actions today?

Today I gave of my time ___, talent ___, treasure ___, and touch ___.

Who did I help today?

What am I grateful for today?

Who needs my prayers today?

God, forgive me where I have been resentful, selfish, dishonest, or afraid today. Help me not to keep anything to myself, but to discuss it openly with another person. Show me where I owe an apology and help me make it, and help me to be kind and loving to all people. Use me in the mainstream of life, and remove worry, remorse, and morbid reflection that I may be of service to others. Amen.

When I retire at night…   /   /

Chronology of today's events:

Was I resentful?
    1. *Who/what*   3. *Affects*

    2. *Cause*   4. *My part*

Was I selfish?

Was I dishonest?

Was I afraid?

Do I owe an apology?

What have I wrongly kept secret?

Was I kind and loving toward all?

What could I have done better?

How did faith or fear rule my actions today?

Today I gave of my time ___, talent ___, treasure ___, and touch ___.

Who did I help today?

What am I grateful for today?

Who needs my prayers today?

God, forgive me where I have been resentful, selfish, dishonest, or afraid today. Help me not to keep anything to myself, but to discuss it openly with another person. Show me where I owe an apology and help me make it, and help me to be kind and loving to all people. Use me in the mainstream of life, and remove worry, remorse, and morbid reflection that I may be of service to others. Amen.

When I retire at night...   /   /

Chronology of today's events:

Was I resentful?
    1. *Who/what*   3. *Affects*

    2. *Cause*   4. *My part*

Was I selfish?

Was I dishonest?

Was I afraid?

Do I owe an apology?

What have I wrongly kept secret?

Was I kind and loving toward all?

What could I have done better?

How did faith or fear rule my actions today?

Today I gave of my time ____, talent ____, treasure ____, and touch ____.

Who did I help today?

What am I grateful for today?

Who needs my prayers today?

God, forgive me where I have been resentful, selfish, dishonest, or afraid today. Help me not to keep anything to myself, but to discuss it openly with another person. Show me where I owe an apology and help me make it, and help me to be kind and loving to all people. Use me in the mainstream of life, and remove worry, remorse, and morbid reflection that I may be of service to others. Amen.

When I retire at night...   /   /

Chronology of today's events:

Was I resentful?
    1. *Who/what*   3. *Affects*

    2. *Cause*   4. *My part*

Was I selfish?

Was I dishonest?

Was I afraid?

Do I owe an apology?

What have I wrongly kept secret?

Was I kind and loving toward all?

What could I have done better?

How did faith or fear rule my actions today?

Today I gave of my time ___, talent ___, treasure ___, and touch ___.

Who did I help today?

What am I grateful for today?

Who needs my prayers today?

God, forgive me where I have been resentful, selfish, dishonest, or afraid today. Help me not to keep anything to myself, but to discuss it openly with another person. Show me where I owe an apology and help me make it, and help me to be kind and loving to all people. Use me in the mainstream of life, and remove worry, remorse, and morbid reflection that I may be of service to others. Amen.

When I retire at night...   /   /

Chronology of today's events:

Was I resentful?
    1. *Who/what*   3.   *Affects*

    2. *Cause*   4.   *My part*

Was I selfish?

Was I dishonest?

Was I afraid?

Do I owe an apology?

What have I wrongly kept secret?

Was I kind and loving toward all?

What could I have done better?

How did faith or fear rule my actions today?

Today I gave of my time ___, talent ___, treasure ___, and touch ___.

Who did I help today?

What am I grateful for today?

Who needs my prayers today?

God, forgive me where I have been resentful, selfish, dishonest, or afraid today. Help me not to keep anything to myself, but to discuss it openly with another person. Show me where I owe an apology and help me make it, and help me to be kind and loving to all people. Use me in the mainstream of life, and remove worry, remorse, and morbid reflection that I may be of service to others. Amen.

When I retire at night...   /   /

Chronology of today's events:

Was I resentful?
    1. *Who/what*   3. *Affects*

    2. *Cause*   4. *My part*

Was I selfish?

Was I dishonest?

Was I afraid?

Do I owe an apology?

What have I wrongly kept secret?

Was I kind and loving toward all?

What could I have done better?

How did faith or fear rule my actions today?

Today I gave of my time ___, talent ___, treasure ___, and touch ___.

Who did I help today?

What am I grateful for today?

Who needs my prayers today?

God, forgive me where I have been resentful, selfish, dishonest, or afraid today. Help me not to keep anything to myself, but to discuss it openly with another person. Show me where I owe an apology and help me make it, and help me to be kind and loving to all people. Use me in the mainstream of life, and remove worry, remorse, and morbid reflection that I may be of service to others. Amen.

When I retire at night...   /   /

Chronology of today's events:

Was I resentful?
    1. Who/what　　　　　　　 *3. Affects*

    2. Cause　　　　　　　　　 *4. My part*

Was I selfish?

Was I dishonest?

Was I afraid?

Do I owe an apology?

What have I wrongly kept secret?

Was I kind and loving toward all?

What could I have done better?

How did faith or fear rule my actions today?

Today I gave of my time ___, talent ___, treasure ___, and touch ___.

Who did I help today?

What am I grateful for today?

Who needs my prayers today?

God, forgive me where I have been resentful, selfish, dishonest, or afraid today. Help me not to keep anything to myself, but to discuss it openly with another person. Show me where I owe an apology and help me make it, and help me to be kind and loving to all people. Use me in the mainstream of life, and remove worry, remorse, and morbid reflection that I may be of service to others. Amen.

When I retire at night...   /   /

Chronology of today's events:

Was I resentful?
    1. *Who/what*   3. *Affects*

    2. *Cause*   4. *My part*

Was I selfish?

Was I dishonest?

Was I afraid?

Do I owe an apology?

What have I wrongly kept secret?

Was I kind and loving toward all?

What could I have done better?

How did faith or fear rule my actions today?

Today I gave of my time ___, talent ___, treasure ___, and touch ___.

Who did I help today?

What am I grateful for today?

Who needs my prayers today?

God, forgive me where I have been resentful, selfish, dishonest, or afraid today. Help me not to keep anything to myself, but to discuss it openly with another person. Show me where I owe an apology and help me make it, and help me to be kind and loving to all people. Use me in the mainstream of life, and remove worry, remorse, and morbid reflection that I may be of service to others. Amen.

When I retire at night...   /   /

Chronology of today's events:

Was I resentful?
    1. *Who/what*   3. *Affects*

    2. *Cause*   4. *My part*

Was I selfish?

Was I dishonest?

Was I afraid?

Do I owe an apology?

What have I wrongly kept secret?

Was I kind and loving toward all?

What could I have done better?

How did faith or fear rule my actions today?

Today I gave of my time ___, talent ___, treasure ___, and touch ___.

Who did I help today?

What am I grateful for today?

Who needs my prayers today?

God, forgive me where I have been resentful, selfish, dishonest, or afraid today. Help me not to keep anything to myself, but to discuss it openly with another person. Show me where I owe an apology and help me make it, and help me to be kind and loving to all people. Use me in the mainstream of life, and remove worry, remorse, and morbid reflection that I may be of service to others. Amen.

When I retire at night...   /   /

Chronology of today's events:

Was I resentful?
- 1. Who/what
- 2. Cause
- 3. Affects
- 4. My part

Was I selfish?

Was I dishonest?

Was I afraid?

Do I owe an apology?

What have I wrongly kept secret?

Was I kind and loving toward all?

What could I have done better?

How did faith or fear rule my actions today?

Today I gave of my time ___, talent ___, treasure ___, and touch ___.

Who did I help today?

What am I grateful for today?

Who needs my prayers today?

God, forgive me where I have been resentful, selfish, dishonest, or afraid today. Help me not to keep anything to myself, but to discuss it openly with another person. Show me where I owe an apology and help me make it, and help me to be kind and loving to all people. Use me in the mainstream of life, and remove worry, remorse, and morbid reflection that I may be of service to others. Amen.

When I retire at night...   /   /

Chronology of today's events:

Was I resentful?
    1. *Who/what*   3. *Affects*

    2. *Cause*   4. *My part*

Was I selfish?

Was I dishonest?

Was I afraid?

Do I owe an apology?

What have I wrongly kept secret?

Was I kind and loving toward all?

What could I have done better?

How did faith or fear rule my actions today?

Today I gave of my time ___, talent ___, treasure ___, and touch ___.

Who did I help today?

What am I grateful for today?

Who needs my prayers today?

God, forgive me where I have been resentful, selfish, dishonest, or afraid today. Help me not to keep anything to myself, but to discuss it openly with another person. Show me where I owe an apology and help me make it, and help me to be kind and loving to all people. Use me in the mainstream of life, and remove worry, remorse, and morbid reflection that I may be of service to others. Amen.

When I retire at night...   /   /

Chronology of today's events:

Was I resentful?
    1. *Who/what*　　　　　　　　3. *Affects*

    2. *Cause*　　　　　　　　　　4. *My part*

Was I selfish?

Was I dishonest?

Was I afraid?

Do I owe an apology?

What have I wrongly kept secret?

Was I kind and loving toward all?

What could I have done better?

How did faith or fear rule my actions today?

Today I gave of my time ___, talent ___, treasure ___, and touch ___.

Who did I help today?

What am I grateful for today?

Who needs my prayers today?

God, forgive me where I have been resentful, selfish, dishonest, or afraid today. Help me not to keep anything to myself, but to discuss it openly with another person. Show me where I owe an apology and help me make it, and help me to be kind and loving to all people. Use me in the mainstream of life, and remove worry, remorse, and morbid reflection that I may be of service to others. Amen.

When I retire at night...   /   /

Chronology of today's events:

Was I resentful?
    1. *Who/what*   3. *Affects*

    2. *Cause*   4. *My part*

Was I selfish?

Was I dishonest?

Was I afraid?

Do I owe an apology?

What have I wrongly kept secret?

Was I kind and loving toward all?

What could I have done better?

How did faith or fear rule my actions today?

Today I gave of my time ___, talent ___, treasure ___, and touch ___.

Who did I help today?

What am I grateful for today?

Who needs my prayers today?

God, forgive me where I have been resentful, selfish, dishonest, or afraid today. Help me not to keep anything to myself, but to discuss it openly with another person. Show me where I owe an apology and help me make it, and help me to be kind and loving to all people. Use me in the mainstream of life, and remove worry, remorse, and morbid reflection that I may be of service to others. Amen.

When I retire at night...   /   /

Chronology of today's events:

Was I resentful?
    1. *Who/what*   3. *Affects*

    2. *Cause*   4. *My part*

Was I selfish?

Was I dishonest?

Was I afraid?

Do I owe an apology?

What have I wrongly kept secret?

Was I kind and loving toward all?

What could I have done better?

How did faith or fear rule my actions today?

Today I gave of my time ___, talent ___, treasure ___, and touch ___.

Who did I help today?

What am I grateful for today?

Who needs my prayers today?

God, forgive me where I have been resentful, selfish, dishonest, or afraid today. Help me not to keep anything to myself, but to discuss it openly with another person. Show me where I owe an apology and help me make it, and help me to be kind and loving to all people. Use me in the mainstream of life, and remove worry, remorse, and morbid reflection that I may be of service to others. Amen.

When I retire at night...   /   /

Chronology of today's events:

Was I resentful?
1. *Who/what*
2. *Cause*
3. *Affects*
4. *My part*

Was I selfish?

Was I dishonest?

Was I afraid?

Do I owe an apology?

What have I wrongly kept secret?

Was I kind and loving toward all?

What could I have done better?

How did faith or fear rule my actions today?

Today I gave of my time ___, talent ___, treasure ___, and touch ___.

Who did I help today?

What am I grateful for today?

Who needs my prayers today?

God, forgive me where I have been resentful, selfish, dishonest, or afraid today. Help me not to keep anything to myself, but to discuss it openly with another person. Show me where I owe an apology and help me make it, and help me to be kind and loving to all people. Use me in the mainstream of life, and remove worry, remorse, and morbid reflection that I may be of service to others. Amen.

When I retire at night...   /   /

Chronology of today's events:

Was I resentful?
    1. Who/what   3. Affects

    2. Cause   4. My part

Was I selfish?

Was I dishonest?

Was I afraid?

Do I owe an apology?

What have I wrongly kept secret?

Was I kind and loving toward all?

What could I have done better?

How did faith or fear rule my actions today?

Today I gave of my time ___, talent ___, treasure ___, and touch ___.

Who did I help today?

What am I grateful for today?

Who needs my prayers today?

God, forgive me where I have been resentful, selfish, dishonest, or afraid today. Help me not to keep anything to myself, but to discuss it openly with another person. Show me where I owe an apology and help me make it, and help me to be kind and loving to all people. Use me in the mainstream of life, and remove worry, remorse, and morbid reflection that I may be of service to others. Amen.

When I retire at night...   /   /

Chronology of today's events:

Was I resentful?
    1. *Who/what*   3. *Affects*

    2. *Cause*   4. *My part*

Was I selfish?

Was I dishonest?

Was I afraid?

Do I owe an apology?

What have I wrongly kept secret?

Was I kind and loving toward all?

What could I have done better?

How did faith or fear rule my actions today?

Today I gave of my time ___, talent ___, treasure ___, and touch ___.

Who did I help today?

What am I grateful for today?

Who needs my prayers today?

God, forgive me where I have been resentful, selfish, dishonest, or afraid today. Help me not to keep anything to myself, but to discuss it openly with another person. Show me where I owe an apology and help me make it, and help me to be kind and loving to all people. Use me in the mainstream of life, and remove worry, remorse, and morbid reflection that I may be of service to others. Amen.

When I retire at night...   /   /

Chronology of today's events:

Was I resentful?
    1. *Who/what*   3. *Affects*

    2. *Cause*   4. *My part*

Was I selfish?

Was I dishonest?

Was I afraid?

Do I owe an apology?

What have I wrongly kept secret?

Was I kind and loving toward all?

What could I have done better?

How did faith or fear rule my actions today?

Today I gave of my time ___, talent ___, treasure ___, and touch ___.

Who did I help today?

What am I grateful for today?

Who needs my prayers today?

God, forgive me where I have been resentful, selfish, dishonest, or afraid today. Help me not to keep anything to myself, but to discuss it openly with another person. Show me where I owe an apology and help me make it, and help me to be kind and loving to all people. Use me in the mainstream of life, and remove worry, remorse, and morbid reflection that I may be of service to others. Amen.

When I retire at night...   /   /

Chronology of today's events:

Was I resentful?
    1. *Who/what*   3. *Affects*

    2. *Cause*   4. *My part*

Was I selfish?

Was I dishonest?

Was I afraid?

Do I owe an apology?

What have I wrongly kept secret?

Was I kind and loving toward all?

What could I have done better?

How did faith or fear rule my actions today?

Today I gave of my time ___, talent ___, treasure ___, and touch ___.

Who did I help today?

What am I grateful for today?

Who needs my prayers today?

God, forgive me where I have been resentful, selfish, dishonest, or afraid today. Help me not to keep anything to myself, but to discuss it openly with another person. Show me where I owe an apology and help me make it, and help me to be kind and loving to all people. Use me in the mainstream of life, and remove worry, remorse, and morbid reflection that I may be of service to others. Amen.

When I retire at night...   /   /

Chronology of today's events:

Was I resentful?

    1. Who/what   3. Affects

    2. Cause   4. My part

Was I selfish?

Was I dishonest?

Was I afraid?

Do I owe an apology?

What have I wrongly kept secret?

Was I kind and loving toward all?

What could I have done better?

How did faith or fear rule my actions today?

Today I gave of my time ___, talent ___, treasure ___, and touch ___.

Who did I help today?

What am I grateful for today?

Who needs my prayers today?

God, forgive me where I have been resentful, selfish, dishonest, or afraid today. Help me not to keep anything to myself, but to discuss it openly with another person. Show me where I owe an apology and help me make it, and help me to be kind and loving to all people. Use me in the mainstream of life, and remove worry, remorse, and morbid reflection that I may be of service to others. Amen.

When I retire at night...   /   /

Chronology of today's events:

Was I resentful?
    1. Who/what   *3. Affects*

    2. Cause   *4. My part*

Was I selfish?

Was I dishonest?

Was I afraid?

Do I owe an apology?

What have I wrongly kept secret?

Was I kind and loving toward all?

What could I have done better?

How did faith or fear rule my actions today?

Today I gave of my time ___, talent ___, treasure ___, and touch ___.

Who did I help today?

What am I grateful for today?

Who needs my prayers today?

God, forgive me where I have been resentful, selfish, dishonest, or afraid today. Help me not to keep anything to myself, but to discuss it openly with another person. Show me where I owe an apology and help me make it, and help me to be kind and loving to all people. Use me in the mainstream of life, and remove worry, remorse, and morbid reflection that I may be of service to others. Amen.

When I retire at night...   /   /

Chronology of today's events:

Was I resentful?
    1. Who/what   3. Affects

    2. Cause   4. My part

Was I selfish?

Was I dishonest?

Was I afraid?

Do I owe an apology?

What have I wrongly kept secret?

Was I kind and loving toward all?

What could I have done better?

How did faith or fear rule my actions today?

Today I gave of my time ___, talent ___, treasure ___, and touch ___.

Who did I help today?

What am I grateful for today?

Who needs my prayers today?

God, forgive me where I have been resentful, selfish, dishonest, or afraid today. Help me not to keep anything to myself, but to discuss it openly with another person. Show me where I owe an apology and help me make it, and help me to be kind and loving to all people. Use me in the mainstream of life, and remove worry, remorse, and morbid reflection that I may be of service to others. Amen.

When I retire at night...   / /

Chronology of today's events:

Was I resentful?
    1. *Who/what*   3. *Affects*

    2. *Cause*   4. *My part*

Was I selfish?

Was I dishonest?

Was I afraid?

Do I owe an apology?

What have I wrongly kept secret?

Was I kind and loving toward all?

What could I have done better?

How did faith or fear rule my actions today?

Today I gave of my time ___, talent ___, treasure ___, and touch ___.

Who did I help today?

What am I grateful for today?

Who needs my prayers today?

God, forgive me where I have been resentful, selfish, dishonest, or afraid today. Help me not to keep anything to myself, but to discuss it openly with another person. Show me where I owe an apology and help me make it, and help me to be kind and loving to all people. Use me in the mainstream of life, and remove worry, remorse, and morbid reflection that I may be of service to others. Amen.

When I retire at night...   /   /

Chronology of today's events:
_____
_____
_____

Was I resentful?
    1. *Who/what*   3. *Affects*

    2. *Cause*   4. *My part*

Was I selfish?
_____
Was I dishonest?
_____
Was I afraid?
_____
Do I owe an apology?
_____
What have I wrongly kept secret?
_____
Was I kind and loving toward all?
_____
What could I have done better?
_____
How did faith or fear rule my actions today?
_____
Today I gave of my time ___, talent ___, treasure ___, and touch ___.
_____
Who did I help today?
_____
What am I grateful for today?
_____
Who needs my prayers today?
_____

God, forgive me where I have been resentful, selfish, dishonest, or afraid today. Help me not to keep anything to myself, but to discuss it openly with another person. Show me where I owe an apology and help me make it, and help me to be kind and loving to all people. Use me in the mainstream of life, and remove worry, remorse, and morbid reflection that I may be of service to others. Amen.

When I retire at night...   /   /

Chronology of today's events:

Was I resentful?
    1. *Who/what*   3. *Affects*

    2. *Cause*   4. *My part*

Was I selfish?

Was I dishonest?

Was I afraid?

Do I owe an apology?

What have I wrongly kept secret?

Was I kind and loving toward all?

What could I have done better?

How did faith or fear rule my actions today?

Today I gave of my time ___, talent ___, treasure ___, and touch ___.

Who did I help today?

What am I grateful for today?

Who needs my prayers today?

God, forgive me where I have been resentful, selfish, dishonest, or afraid today. Help me not to keep anything to myself, but to discuss it openly with another person. Show me where I owe an apology and help me make it, and help me to be kind and loving to all people. Use me in the mainstream of life, and remove worry, remorse, and morbid reflection that I may be of service to others. Amen.

When I retire at night...   /   /

Chronology of today's events:

Was I resentful?
   1. Who/what   3. Affects

   2. Cause   4. My part

Was I selfish?

Was I dishonest?

Was I afraid?

Do I owe an apology?

What have I wrongly kept secret?

Was I kind and loving toward all?

What could I have done better?

How did faith or fear rule my actions today?

Today I gave of my time ___, talent ___, treasure ___, and touch ___.

Who did I help today?

What am I grateful for today?

Who needs my prayers today?

God, forgive me where I have been resentful, selfish, dishonest, or afraid today. Help me not to keep anything to myself, but to discuss it openly with another person. Show me where I owe an apology and help me make it, and help me to be kind and loving to all people. Use me in the mainstream of life, and remove worry, remorse, and morbid reflection that I may be of service to others. Amen.

When I retire at night...   /   /

Chronology of today's events:

Was I resentful?
    1. *Who/what*   3. *Affects*

    2. *Cause*   4. *My part*

Was I selfish?

Was I dishonest?

Was I afraid?

Do I owe an apology?

What have I wrongly kept secret?

Was I kind and loving toward all?

What could I have done better?

How did faith or fear rule my actions today?

Today I gave of my time ___, talent ___, treasure ___, and touch ___.

Who did I help today?

What am I grateful for today?

Who needs my prayers today?

God, forgive me where I have been resentful, selfish, dishonest, or afraid today. Help me not to keep anything to myself, but to discuss it openly with another person. Show me where I owe an apology and help me make it, and help me to be kind and loving to all people. Use me in the mainstream of life, and remove worry, remorse, and morbid reflection that I may be of service to others. Amen.

When I retire at night...   /   /

Chronology of today's events:

Was I resentful?
    1. Who/what   3.   Affects

    2. Cause   4.   My part

Was I selfish?

Was I dishonest?

Was I afraid?

Do I owe an apology?

What have I wrongly kept secret?

Was I kind and loving toward all?

What could I have done better?

How did faith or fear rule my actions today?

Today I gave of my time ___, talent ___, treasure ___, and touch ___.

Who did I help today?

What am I grateful for today?

Who needs my prayers today?

God, forgive me where I have been resentful, selfish, dishonest, or afraid today. Help me not to keep anything to myself, but to discuss it openly with another person. Show me where I owe an apology and help me make it, and help me to be kind and loving to all people. Use me in the mainstream of life, and remove worry, remorse, and morbid reflection that I may be of service to others. Amen.

When I retire at night...   /   /

Chronology of today's events:

Was I resentful?

    1. *Who/what*   3. *Affects*

    2. *Cause*   4. *My part*

Was I selfish?

Was I dishonest?

Was I afraid?

Do I owe an apology?

What have I wrongly kept secret?

Was I kind and loving toward all?

What could I have done better?

How did faith or fear rule my actions today?

Today I gave of my time ___, talent ___, treasure ___, and touch ___.

Who did I help today?

What am I grateful for today?

Who needs my prayers today?

God, forgive me where I have been resentful, selfish, dishonest, or afraid today. Help me not to keep anything to myself, but to discuss it openly with another person. Show me where I owe an apology and help me make it, and help me to be kind and loving to all people. Use me in the mainstream of life, and remove worry, remorse, and morbid reflection that I may be of service to others. Amen.

When I retire at night...   /   /

Chronology of today's events:

Was I resentful?
    1. *Who/what*　　　　　　　　3. *Affects*

    2. *Cause*　　　　　　　　　　4. *My part*

Was I selfish?

Was I dishonest?

Was I afraid?

Do I owe an apology?

What have I wrongly kept secret?

Was I kind and loving toward all?

What could I have done better?

How did faith or fear rule my actions today?

Today I gave of my time ___, talent ___, treasure ___, and touch ___.

Who did I help today?

What am I grateful for today?

Who needs my prayers today?

God, forgive me where I have been resentful, selfish, dishonest, or afraid today. Help me not to keep anything to myself, but to discuss it openly with another person. Show me where I owe an apology and help me make it, and help me to be kind and loving to all people. Use me in the mainstream of life, and remove worry, remorse, and morbid reflection that I may be of service to others. Amen.

When I retire at night...   /   /

Chronology of today's events:
_____
_____

Was I resentful?
    1. *Who/what*   3.   *Affects*

    2. *Cause*   4.   *My part*

Was I selfish?

Was I dishonest?

Was I afraid?

Do I owe an apology?

What have I wrongly kept secret?

Was I kind and loving toward all?

What could I have done better?

How did faith or fear rule my actions today?

Today I gave of my time ___, talent ___, treasure ___, and touch ___.

Who did I help today?

What am I grateful for today?

Who needs my prayers today?

God, forgive me where I have been resentful, selfish, dishonest, or afraid today. Help me not to keep anything to myself, but to discuss it openly with another person. Show me where I owe an apology and help me make it, and help me to be kind and loving to all people. Use me in the mainstream of life, and remove worry, remorse, and morbid reflection that I may be of service to others. Amen.

When I retire at night…   /   /

Chronology of today's events:

Was I resentful?
    1. Who/what
    2. Cause
    3. Affects
    4. My part

Was I selfish?

Was I dishonest?

Was I afraid?

Do I owe an apology?

What have I wrongly kept secret?

Was I kind and loving toward all?

What could I have done better?

How did faith or fear rule my actions today?

Today I gave of my time ___, talent ___, treasure ___, and touch ___.

Who did I help today?

What am I grateful for today?

Who needs my prayers today?

God, forgive me where I have been resentful, selfish, dishonest, or afraid today. Help me not to keep anything to myself, but to discuss it openly with another person. Show me where I owe an apology and help me make it, and help me to be kind and loving to all people. Use me in the mainstream of life, and remove worry, remorse, and morbid reflection that I may be of service to others. Amen.

When I retire at night...   /   /

Chronology of today's events:

Was I resentful?
1. *Who/what*   3. *Affects*
2. *Cause*   4. *My part*

Was I selfish?

Was I dishonest?

Was I afraid?

Do I owe an apology?

What have I wrongly kept secret?

Was I kind and loving toward all?

What could I have done better?

How did faith or fear rule my actions today?

Today I gave of my time ___, talent ___, treasure ___, and touch ___.

Who did I help today?

What am I grateful for today?

Who needs my prayers today?

God, forgive me where I have been resentful, selfish, dishonest, or afraid today. Help me not to keep anything to myself, but to discuss it openly with another person. Show me where I owe an apology and help me make it, and help me to be kind and loving to all people. Use me in the mainstream of life, and remove worry, remorse, and morbid reflection that I may be of service to others. Amen.

When I retire at night...   /   /

Chronology of today's events:

Was I resentful?
    1. Who/what   3. Affects

    2. Cause   4. My part

Was I selfish?

Was I dishonest?

Was I afraid?

Do I owe an apology?

What have I wrongly kept secret?

Was I kind and loving toward all?

What could I have done better?

How did faith or fear rule my actions today?

Today I gave of my time ___, talent ___, treasure ___, and touch ___.

Who did I help today?

What am I grateful for today?

Who needs my prayers today?

God, forgive me where I have been resentful, selfish, dishonest, or afraid today. Help me not to keep anything to myself, but to discuss it openly with another person. Show me where I owe an apology and help me make it, and help me to be kind and loving to all people. Use me in the mainstream of life, and remove worry, remorse, and morbid reflection that I may be of service to others. Amen.

When I retire at night...   /   /

Chronology of today's events:

Was I resentful?
    1. *Who/what*   3. *Affects*

    2. *Cause*   4. *My part*

Was I selfish?

Was I dishonest?

Was I afraid?

Do I owe an apology?

What have I wrongly kept secret?

Was I kind and loving toward all?

What could I have done better?

How did faith or fear rule my actions today?

Today I gave of my time ___, talent ___, treasure ___, and touch ___.

Who did I help today?

What am I grateful for today?

Who needs my prayers today?

God, forgive me where I have been resentful, selfish, dishonest, or afraid today. Help me not to keep anything to myself, but to discuss it openly with another person. Show me where I owe an apology and help me make it, and help me to be kind and loving to all people. Use me in the mainstream of life, and remove worry, remorse, and morbid reflection that I may be of service to others. Amen.

When I retire at night…   /   /

Chronology of today's events:

Was I resentful?
1. *Who/what*   3. *Affects*
2. *Cause*   4. *My part*

Was I selfish?

Was I dishonest?

Was I afraid?

Do I owe an apology?

What have I wrongly kept secret?

Was I kind and loving toward all?

What could I have done better?

How did faith or fear rule my actions today?

Today I gave of my time ___, talent ___, treasure ___, and touch ___.

Who did I help today?

What am I grateful for today?

Who needs my prayers today?

God, forgive me where I have been resentful, selfish, dishonest, or afraid today. Help me not to keep anything to myself, but to discuss it openly with another person. Show me where I owe an apology and help me make it, and help me to be kind and loving to all people. Use me in the mainstream of life, and remove worry, remorse, and morbid reflection that I may be of service to others. Amen.

When I retire at night...   /   /

Chronology of today's events:

Was I resentful?
    1. *Who/what*　　　　　　　　3. *Affects*

    2. *Cause*　　　　　　　　　　4. *My part*

Was I selfish?

Was I dishonest?

Was I afraid?

Do I owe an apology?

What have I wrongly kept secret?

Was I kind and loving toward all?

What could I have done better?

How did faith or fear rule my actions today?

Today I gave of my time ___, talent ___, treasure ___, and touch ___.

Who did I help today?

What am I grateful for today?

Who needs my prayers today?

God, forgive me where I have been resentful, selfish, dishonest, or afraid today. Help me not to keep anything to myself, but to discuss it openly with another person. Show me where I owe an apology and help me make it, and help me to be kind and loving to all people. Use me in the mainstream of life, and remove worry, remorse, and morbid reflection that I may be of service to others. Amen.

When I retire at night...   /   /

Chronology of today's events:

Was I resentful?

   1. *Who/what*   3. *Affects*

   2. *Cause*   4. *My part*

Was I selfish?

Was I dishonest?

Was I afraid?

Do I owe an apology?

What have I wrongly kept secret?

Was I kind and loving toward all?

What could I have done better?

How did faith or fear rule my actions today?

Today I gave of my time ___, talent ___, treasure ___, and touch ___.

Who did I help today?

What am I grateful for today?

Who needs my prayers today?

God, forgive me where I have been resentful, selfish, dishonest, or afraid today. Help me not to keep anything to myself, but to discuss it openly with another person. Show me where I owe an apology and help me make it, and help me to be kind and loving to all people. Use me in the mainstream of life, and remove worry, remorse, and morbid reflection that I may be of service to others. Amen.

When I retire at night...   /   /

Chronology of today's events:

Was I resentful?
    1. *Who/what*   3. *Affects*

    2. *Cause*   4. *My part*

Was I selfish?

Was I dishonest?

Was I afraid?

Do I owe an apology?

What have I wrongly kept secret?

Was I kind and loving toward all?

What could I have done better?

How did faith or fear rule my actions today?

Today I gave of my time ___, talent ___, treasure ___, and touch ___.

Who did I help today?

What am I grateful for today?

Who needs my prayers today?

God, forgive me where I have been resentful, selfish, dishonest, or afraid today. Help me not to keep anything to myself, but to discuss it openly with another person. Show me where I owe an apology and help me make it, and help me to be kind and loving to all people. Use me in the mainstream of life, and remove worry, remorse, and morbid reflection that I may be of service to others. Amen.

When I retire at night...   /   /

Chronology of today's events:

Was I resentful?
    1. Who/what   3. Affects

    2. Cause   4. My part

Was I selfish?

Was I dishonest?

Was I afraid?

Do I owe an apology?

What have I wrongly kept secret?

Was I kind and loving toward all?

What could I have done better?

How did faith or fear rule my actions today?

Today I gave of my time ___, talent ___, treasure ___, and touch ___.

Who did I help today?

What am I grateful for today?

Who needs my prayers today?

God, forgive me where I have been resentful, selfish, dishonest, or afraid today. Help me not to keep anything to myself, but to discuss it openly with another person. Show me where I owe an apology and help me make it, and help me to be kind and loving to all people. Use me in the mainstream of life, and remove worry, remorse, and morbid reflection that I may be of service to others. Amen.

When I retire at night...   /   /

Chronology of today's events:

Was I resentful?
    1. *Who/what*   3. *Affects*

    2. *Cause*   4. *My part*

Was I selfish?

Was I dishonest?

Was I afraid?

Do I owe an apology?

What have I wrongly kept secret?

Was I kind and loving toward all?

What could I have done better?

How did faith or fear rule my actions today?

Today I gave of my time ___, talent ___, treasure ___, and touch ___.

Who did I help today?

What am I grateful for today?

Who needs my prayers today?

God, forgive me where I have been resentful, selfish, dishonest, or afraid today. Help me not to keep anything to myself, but to discuss it openly with another person. Show me where I owe an apology and help me make it, and help me to be kind and loving to all people. Use me in the mainstream of life, and remove worry, remorse, and morbid reflection that I may be of service to others. Amen.

When I retire at night...   /   /

Chronology of today's events:

Was I resentful?
    1. *Who/what*   3. *Affects*

    2. *Cause*   4. *My part*

Was I selfish?

Was I dishonest?

Was I afraid?

Do I owe an apology?

What have I wrongly kept secret?

Was I kind and loving toward all?

What could I have done better?

How did faith or fear rule my actions today?

Today I gave of my time ___, talent ___, treasure ___, and touch ___.

Who did I help today?

What am I grateful for today?

Who needs my prayers today?

God, forgive me where I have been resentful, selfish, dishonest, or afraid today. Help me not to keep anything to myself, but to discuss it openly with another person. Show me where I owe an apology and help me make it, and help me to be kind and loving to all people. Use me in the mainstream of life, and remove worry, remorse, and morbid reflection that I may be of service to others. Amen.

When I retire at night...   / /

Chronology of today's events:

Was I resentful?
1. *Who/what*
2. *Cause*
3. *Affects*
4. *My part*

Was I selfish?

Was I dishonest?

Was I afraid?

Do I owe an apology?

What have I wrongly kept secret?

Was I kind and loving toward all?

What could I have done better?

How did faith or fear rule my actions today?

Today I gave of my time ___, talent ___, treasure ___, and touch ___.

Who did I help today?

What am I grateful for today?

Who needs my prayers today?

God, forgive me where I have been resentful, selfish, dishonest, or afraid today. Help me not to keep anything to myself, but to discuss it openly with another person. Show me where I owe an apology and help me make it, and help me to be kind and loving to all people. Use me in the mainstream of life, and remove worry, remorse, and morbid reflection that I may be of service to others. Amen.

When I retire at night...   /   /

Chronology of today's events:

Was I resentful?
   1. Who/what   3. Affects

   2. Cause   4. My part

Was I selfish?

Was I dishonest?

Was I afraid?

Do I owe an apology?

What have I wrongly kept secret?

Was I kind and loving toward all?

What could I have done better?

How did faith or fear rule my actions today?

Today I gave of my time ___, talent ___, treasure ___, and touch ___.

Who did I help today?

What am I grateful for today?

Who needs my prayers today?

God, forgive me where I have been resentful, selfish, dishonest, or afraid today. Help me not to keep anything to myself, but to discuss it openly with another person. Show me where I owe an apology and help me make it, and help me to be kind and loving to all people. Use me in the mainstream of life, and remove worry, remorse, and morbid reflection that I may be of service to others. Amen.

When I retire at night...   /   /

Chronology of today's events:

Was I resentful?
- 1. *Who/what*
- 2. *Cause*
- 3. *Affects*
- 4. *My part*

Was I selfish?

Was I dishonest?

Was I afraid?

Do I owe an apology?

What have I wrongly kept secret?

Was I kind and loving toward all?

What could I have done better?

How did faith or fear rule my actions today?

Today I gave of my time ___, talent ___, treasure ___, and touch ___.

Who did I help today?

What am I grateful for today?

Who needs my prayers today?

God, forgive me where I have been resentful, selfish, dishonest, or afraid today. Help me not to keep anything to myself, but to discuss it openly with another person. Show me where I owe an apology and help me make it, and help me to be kind and loving to all people. Use me in the mainstream of life, and remove worry, remorse, and morbid reflection that I may be of service to others. Amen.

When I retire at night...   /   /

Chronology of today's events:

Was I resentful?
 1. *Who/what*   3. *Affects*
 2. *Cause*   4. *My part*

Was I selfish?

Was I dishonest?

Was I afraid?

Do I owe an apology?

What have I wrongly kept secret?

Was I kind and loving toward all?

What could I have done better?

How did faith or fear rule my actions today?

Today I gave of my time ___, talent ___, treasure ___, and touch ___.

Who did I help today?

What am I grateful for today?

Who needs my prayers today?

God, forgive me where I have been resentful, selfish, dishonest, or afraid today. Help me not to keep anything to myself, but to discuss it openly with another person. Show me where I owe an apology and help me make it, and help me to be kind and loving to all people. Use me in the mainstream of life, and remove worry, remorse, and morbid reflection that I may be of service to others. Amen.

When I retire at night...   /   /

Chronology of today's events:

Was I resentful?

    1. *Who/what*   3. *Affects*

    2. *Cause*   4. *My part*

Was I selfish?

Was I dishonest?

Was I afraid?

Do I owe an apology?

What have I wrongly kept secret?

Was I kind and loving toward all?

What could I have done better?

How did faith or fear rule my actions today?

Today I gave of my time ___, talent ___, treasure ___, and touch ___.

Who did I help today?

What am I grateful for today?

Who needs my prayers today?

God, forgive me where I have been resentful, selfish, dishonest, or afraid today. Help me not to keep anything to myself, but to discuss it openly with another person. Show me where I owe an apology and help me make it, and help me to be kind and loving to all people. Use me in the mainstream of life, and remove worry, remorse, and morbid reflection that I may be of service to others. Amen.

When I retire at night...   /   /

Chronology of today's events:

Was I resentful?
    1. Who/what   *3. Affects*

    2. Cause   *4. My part*

Was I selfish?

Was I dishonest?

Was I afraid?

Do I owe an apology?

What have I wrongly kept secret?

Was I kind and loving toward all?

What could I have done better?

How did faith or fear rule my actions today?

Today I gave of my time ___, talent ___, treasure ___, and touch ___.

Who did I help today?

What am I grateful for today?

Who needs my prayers today?

God, forgive me where I have been resentful, selfish, dishonest, or afraid today. Help me not to keep anything to myself, but to discuss it openly with another person. Show me where I owe an apology and help me make it, and help me to be kind and loving to all people. Use me in the mainstream of life, and remove worry, remorse, and morbid reflection that I may be of service to others. Amen.

When I retire at night...   /   /

Chronology of today's events:

Was I resentful?
    1. *Who/what*   3. *Affects*

    2. *Cause*   4. *My part*

Was I selfish?

Was I dishonest?

Was I afraid?

Do I owe an apology?

What have I wrongly kept secret?

Was I kind and loving toward all?

What could I have done better?

How did faith or fear rule my actions today?

Today I gave of my time ___, talent ___, treasure ___, and touch ___.

Who did I help today?

What am I grateful for today?

Who needs my prayers today?

God, forgive me where I have been resentful, selfish, dishonest, or afraid today. Help me not to keep anything to myself, but to discuss it openly with another person. Show me where I owe an apology and help me make it, and help me to be kind and loving to all people. Use me in the mainstream of life, and remove worry, remorse, and morbid reflection that I may be of service to others. Amen.

When I retire at night...   /   /

Chronology of today's events:

Was I resentful?
    1. *Who / what*   3. *Affects*

    2. *Cause*   4. *My part*

Was I selfish?

Was I dishonest?

Was I afraid?

Do I owe an apology?

What have I wrongly kept secret?

Was I kind and loving toward all?

What could I have done better?

How did faith or fear rule my actions today?

Today I gave of my time ___, talent ___, treasure ___, and touch ___.

Who did I help today?

What am I grateful for today?

Who needs my prayers today?

God, forgive me where I have been resentful, selfish, dishonest, or afraid today. Help me not to keep anything to myself, but to discuss it openly with another person. Show me where I owe an apology and help me make it, and help me to be kind and loving to all people. Use me in the mainstream of life, and remove worry, remorse, and morbid reflection that I may be of service to others. Amen.

When I retire at night...   /   /

Chronology of today's events:

Was I resentful?
    1. Who/what   3. Affects

    2. Cause   4. My part

Was I selfish?

Was I dishonest?

Was I afraid?

Do I owe an apology?

What have I wrongly kept secret?

Was I kind and loving toward all?

What could I have done better?

How did faith or fear rule my actions today?

Today I gave of my time ___, talent ___, treasure ___, and touch ___.

Who did I help today?

What am I grateful for today?

Who needs my prayers today?

God, forgive me where I have been resentful, selfish, dishonest, or afraid today. Help me not to keep anything to myself, but to discuss it openly with another person. Show me where I owe an apology and help me make it, and help me to be kind and loving to all people. Use me in the mainstream of life, and remove worry, remorse, and morbid reflection that I may be of service to others. Amen.

When I retire at night...   /   /

Chronology of today's events:

Was I resentful?
    1. Who/what   *3. Affects*

    2. Cause   *4. My part*

Was I selfish?

Was I dishonest?

Was I afraid?

Do I owe an apology?

What have I wrongly kept secret?

Was I kind and loving toward all?

What could I have done better?

How did faith or fear rule my actions today?

Today I gave of my time ___, talent ___, treasure ___, and touch ___.

Who did I help today?

What am I grateful for today?

Who needs my prayers today?

God, forgive me where I have been resentful, selfish, dishonest, or afraid today. Help me not to keep anything to myself, but to discuss it openly with another person. Show me where I owe an apology and help me make it, and help me to be kind and loving to all people. Use me in the mainstream of life, and remove worry, remorse, and morbid reflection that I may be of service to others. Amen.

When I retire at night...   /   /

Chronology of today's events:

Was I resentful?
    1. *Who/what*   3. *Affects*

    2. *Cause*   4. *My part*

Was I selfish?

Was I dishonest?

Was I afraid?

Do I owe an apology?

What have I wrongly kept secret?

Was I kind and loving toward all?

What could I have done better?

How did faith or fear rule my actions today?

Today I gave of my time ___, talent ___, treasure ___, and touch ___.

Who did I help today?

What am I grateful for today?

Who needs my prayers today?

God, forgive me where I have been resentful, selfish, dishonest, or afraid today. Help me not to keep anything to myself, but to discuss it openly with another person. Show me where I owe an apology and help me make it, and help me to be kind and loving to all people. Use me in the mainstream of life, and remove worry, remorse, and morbid reflection that I may be of service to others. Amen.

When I retire at night...   /   /

Chronology of today's events:

Was I resentful?
    1. *Who/what*　　　　　　　3. *Affects*

    2. *Cause*　　　　　　　　　4. *My part*

Was I selfish?

Was I dishonest?

Was I afraid?

Do I owe an apology?

What have I wrongly kept secret?

Was I kind and loving toward all?

What could I have done better?

How did faith or fear rule my actions today?

Today I gave of my time ____, talent ____, treasure ____, and touch ____.

Who did I help today?

What am I grateful for today?

Who needs my prayers today?

God, forgive me where I have been resentful, selfish, dishonest, or afraid today. Help me not to keep anything to myself, but to discuss it openly with another person. Show me where I owe an apology and help me make it, and help me to be kind and loving to all people. Use me in the mainstream of life, and remove worry, remorse, and morbid reflection that I may be of service to others. Amen.

When I retire at night...   /   /

Chronology of today's events:

Was I resentful?
    1. *Who/what*   3. *Affects*

    2. *Cause*   4. *My part*

Was I selfish?

Was I dishonest?

Was I afraid?

Do I owe an apology?

What have I wrongly kept secret?

Was I kind and loving toward all?

What could I have done better?

How did faith or fear rule my actions today?

Today I gave of my time ___, talent ___, treasure ___, and touch ___.

Who did I help today?

What am I grateful for today?

Who needs my prayers today?

God, forgive me where I have been resentful, selfish, dishonest, or afraid today. Help me not to keep anything to myself, but to discuss it openly with another person. Show me where I owe an apology and help me make it, and help me to be kind and loving to all people. Use me in the mainstream of life, and remove worry, remorse, and morbid reflection that I may be of service to others. Amen.

When I retire at night...   / /

Chronology of today's events:

Was I resentful?
   1. *Who/what*
   2. *Cause*
   3. *Affects*
   4. *My part*

Was I selfish?

Was I dishonest?

Was I afraid?

Do I owe an apology?

What have I wrongly kept secret?

Was I kind and loving toward all?

What could I have done better?

How did faith or fear rule my actions today?

Today I gave of my time ___, talent ___, treasure ___, and touch ___.

Who did I help today?

What am I grateful for today?

Who needs my prayers today?

God, forgive me where I have been resentful, selfish, dishonest, or afraid today. Help me not to keep anything to myself, but to discuss it openly with another person. Show me where I owe an apology and help me make it, and help me to be kind and loving to all people. Use me in the mainstream of life, and remove worry, remorse, and morbid reflection that I may be of service to others. Amen.

When I retire at night...   /   /

Chronology of today's events:

Was I resentful?
1. *Who/what*
2. *Cause*
3. *Affects*
4. *My part*

Was I selfish?

Was I dishonest?

Was I afraid?

Do I owe an apology?

What have I wrongly kept secret?

Was I kind and loving toward all?

What could I have done better?

How did faith or fear rule my actions today?

Today I gave of my time ___, talent ___, treasure ___, and touch ___.

Who did I help today?

What am I grateful for today?

Who needs my prayers today?

God, forgive me where I have been resentful, selfish, dishonest, or afraid today. Help me not to keep anything to myself, but to discuss it openly with another person. Show me where I owe an apology and help me make it, and help me to be kind and loving to all people. Use me in the mainstream of life, and remove worry, remorse, and morbid reflection that I may be of service to others. Amen.

When I retire at night...   /   /

Chronology of today's events:

Was I resentful?
    1. *Who/what*   3. *Affects*

    2. *Cause*   4. *My part*

Was I selfish?

Was I dishonest?

Was I afraid?

Do I owe an apology?

What have I wrongly kept secret?

Was I kind and loving toward all?

What could I have done better?

How did faith or fear rule my actions today?

Today I gave of my time ___, talent ___, treasure ___, and touch ___.

Who did I help today?

What am I grateful for today?

Who needs my prayers today?

God, forgive me where I have been resentful, selfish, dishonest, or afraid today. Help me not to keep anything to myself, but to discuss it openly with another person. Show me where I owe an apology and help me make it, and help me to be kind and loving to all people. Use me in the mainstream of life, and remove worry, remorse, and morbid reflection that I may be of service to others. Amen.

When I retire at night...   /   /

Chronology of today's events:

Was I resentful?
    1. *Who/what*   3. *Affects*

    2. *Cause*   4. *My part*

Was I selfish?

Was I dishonest?

Was I afraid?

Do I owe an apology?

What have I wrongly kept secret?

Was I kind and loving toward all?

What could I have done better?

How did faith or fear rule my actions today?

Today I gave of my time ___, talent ___, treasure ___, and touch ___.

Who did I help today?

What am I grateful for today?

Who needs my prayers today?

God, forgive me where I have been resentful, selfish, dishonest, or afraid today. Help me not to keep anything to myself, but to discuss it openly with another person. Show me where I owe an apology and help me make it, and help me to be kind and loving to all people. Use me in the mainstream of life, and remove worry, remorse, and morbid reflection that I may be of service to others. Amen.

When I retire at night...   /   /

Chronology of today's events:

_____
_____
_____

Was I resentful?
    1. *Who/what*   3. *Affects*

    2. *Cause*   4. *My part*

Was I selfish?

Was I dishonest?

Was I afraid?

Do I owe an apology?

What have I wrongly kept secret?

Was I kind and loving toward all?

What could I have done better?

How did faith or fear rule my actions today?

Today I gave of my time ___, talent ___, treasure ___, and touch ___.

Who did I help today?

What am I grateful for today?

Who needs my prayers today?

God, forgive me where I have been resentful, selfish, dishonest, or afraid today. Help me not to keep anything to myself, but to discuss it openly with another person. Show me where I owe an apology and help me make it, and help me to be kind and loving to all people. Use me in the mainstream of life, and remove worry, remorse, and morbid reflection that I may be of service to others. Amen.

When I retire at night...   /   /

Chronology of today's events:

Was I resentful?
    1. Who / what　　　　　　*3. Affects*

    2. Cause　　　　　　　　*4. My part*

Was I selfish?

Was I dishonest?

Was I afraid?

Do I owe an apology?

What have I wrongly kept secret?

Was I kind and loving toward all?

What could I have done better?

How did faith or fear rule my actions today?

Today I gave of my time ___, talent ___, treasure ___, and touch ___.

Who did I help today?

What am I grateful for today?

Who needs my prayers today?

God, forgive me where I have been resentful, selfish, dishonest, or afraid today. Help me not to keep anything to myself, but to discuss it openly with another person. Show me where I owe an apology and help me make it, and help me to be kind and loving to all people. Use me in the mainstream of life, and remove worry, remorse, and morbid reflection that I may be of service to others. Amen.

When I retire at night...   /   /

Chronology of today's events:

Was I resentful?
    1. Who/what   3. Affects

    2. Cause   4. My part

Was I selfish?

Was I dishonest?

Was I afraid?

Do I owe an apology?

What have I wrongly kept secret?

Was I kind and loving toward all?

What could I have done better?

How did faith or fear rule my actions today?

Today I gave of my time ___, talent ___, treasure ___, and touch ___.

Who did I help today?

What am I grateful for today?

Who needs my prayers today?

God, forgive me where I have been resentful, selfish, dishonest, or afraid today. Help me not to keep anything to myself, but to discuss it openly with another person. Show me where I owe an apology and help me make it, and help me to be kind and loving to all people. Use me in the mainstream of life, and remove worry, remorse, and morbid reflection that I may be of service to others. Amen.

When I retire at night...   /   /

Chronology of today's events:

Was I resentful?

    1. *Who/what*　　　　　　　3. *Affects*

    2. *Cause*　　　　　　　　　4. *My part*

Was I selfish?

Was I dishonest?

Was I afraid?

Do I owe an apology?

What have I wrongly kept secret?

Was I kind and loving toward all?

What could I have done better?

How did faith or fear rule my actions today?

Today I gave of my time ___, talent ___, treasure ___, and touch ___.

Who did I help today?

What am I grateful for today?

Who needs my prayers today?

God, forgive me where I have been resentful, selfish, dishonest, or afraid today. Help me not to keep anything to myself, but to discuss it openly with another person. Show me where I owe an apology and help me make it, and help me to be kind and loving to all people. Use me in the mainstream of life, and remove worry, remorse, and morbid reflection that I may be of service to others. Amen.

When I retire at night...   /   /

Chronology of today's events:

Was I resentful?
    1. Who/what   *3. Affects*

    2. Cause   *4. My part*

Was I selfish?

Was I dishonest?

Was I afraid?

Do I owe an apology?

What have I wrongly kept secret?

Was I kind and loving toward all?

What could I have done better?

How did faith or fear rule my actions today?

Today I gave of my time ___, talent ___, treasure ___, and touch ___.

Who did I help today?

What am I grateful for today?

Who needs my prayers today?

God, forgive me where I have been resentful, selfish, dishonest, or afraid today. Help me not to keep anything to myself, but to discuss it openly with another person. Show me where I owe an apology and help me make it, and help me to be kind and loving to all people. Use me in the mainstream of life, and remove worry, remorse, and morbid reflection that I may be of service to others. Amen.

When I retire at night...   /   /

Chronology of today's events:

Was I resentful?
    1. Who/what   3. Affects

    2. Cause   4. My part

Was I selfish?

Was I dishonest?

Was I afraid?

Do I owe an apology?

What have I wrongly kept secret?

Was I kind and loving toward all?

What could I have done better?

How did faith or fear rule my actions today?

Today I gave of my time ___, talent ___, treasure ___, and touch ___.

Who did I help today?

What am I grateful for today?

Who needs my prayers today?

God, forgive me where I have been resentful, selfish, dishonest, or afraid today. Help me not to keep anything to myself, but to discuss it openly with another person. Show me where I owe an apology and help me make it, and help me to be kind and loving to all people. Use me in the mainstream of life, and remove worry, remorse, and morbid reflection that I may be of service to others. Amen.

When I retire at night...   /   /

Chronology of today's events:

Was I resentful?
   1. *Who/what*   3. *Affects*

   2. *Cause*   4. *My part*

Was I selfish?

Was I dishonest?

Was I afraid?

Do I owe an apology?

What have I wrongly kept secret?

Was I kind and loving toward all?

What could I have done better?

How did faith or fear rule my actions today?

Today I gave of my time ___, talent ___, treasure ___, and touch ___.

Who did I help today?

What am I grateful for today?

Who needs my prayers today?

God, forgive me where I have been resentful, selfish, dishonest, or afraid today. Help me not to keep anything to myself, but to discuss it openly with another person. Show me where I owe an apology and help me make it, and help me to be kind and loving to all people. Use me in the mainstream of life, and remove worry, remorse, and morbid reflection that I may be of service to others. Amen.

When I retire at night...   /   /

Chronology of today's events:

Was I resentful?
    1. *Who/what*　　　　　　　3. *Affects*

    2. *Cause*　　　　　　　　　4. *My part*

Was I selfish?

Was I dishonest?

Was I afraid?

Do I owe an apology?

What have I wrongly kept secret?

Was I kind and loving toward all?

What could I have done better?

How did faith or fear rule my actions today?

Today I gave of my time ___, talent ___, treasure ___, and touch ___.

Who did I help today?

What am I grateful for today?

Who needs my prayers today?

God, forgive me where I have been resentful, selfish, dishonest, or afraid today. Help me not to keep anything to myself, but to discuss it openly with another person. Show me where I owe an apology and help me make it, and help me to be kind and loving to all people. Use me in the mainstream of life, and remove worry, remorse, and morbid reflection that I may be of service to others. Amen.

When I retire at night...   /   /

Chronology of today's events:

Was I resentful?
    1. Who/what   3. Affects

    2. Cause   4. My part

Was I selfish?

Was I dishonest?

Was I afraid?

Do I owe an apology?

What have I wrongly kept secret?

Was I kind and loving toward all?

What could I have done better?

How did faith or fear rule my actions today?

Today I gave of my time ___, talent ___, treasure ___, and touch ___.

Who did I help today?

What am I grateful for today?

Who needs my prayers today?

God, forgive me where I have been resentful, selfish, dishonest, or afraid today. Help me not to keep anything to myself, but to discuss it openly with another person. Show me where I owe an apology and help me make it, and help me to be kind and loving to all people. Use me in the mainstream of life, and remove worry, remorse, and morbid reflection that I may be of service to others. Amen.

When I retire at night...   /   /

Chronology of today's events:

Was I resentful?
    1. *Who/what*   3. *Affects*

    2. *Cause*   4. *My part*

Was I selfish?

Was I dishonest?

Was I afraid?

Do I owe an apology?

What have I wrongly kept secret?

Was I kind and loving toward all?

What could I have done better?

How did faith or fear rule my actions today?

Today I gave of my time ___, talent ___, treasure ___, and touch ___.

Who did I help today?

What am I grateful for today?

Who needs my prayers today?

God, forgive me where I have been resentful, selfish, dishonest, or afraid today. Help me not to keep anything to myself, but to discuss it openly with another person. Show me where I owe an apology and help me make it, and help me to be kind and loving to all people. Use me in the mainstream of life, and remove worry, remorse, and morbid reflection that I may be of service to others. Amen.

When I retire at night...   /   /

Chronology of today's events:

Was I resentful?
    1. Who/what   *3. Affects*

    2. Cause   *4. My part*

Was I selfish?

Was I dishonest?

Was I afraid?

Do I owe an apology?

What have I wrongly kept secret?

Was I kind and loving toward all?

What could I have done better?

How did faith or fear rule my actions today?

Today I gave of my time ___, talent ___, treasure ___, and touch ___.

Who did I help today?

What am I grateful for today?

Who needs my prayers today?

God, forgive me where I have been resentful, selfish, dishonest, or afraid today. Help me not to keep anything to myself, but to discuss it openly with another person. Show me where I owe an apology and help me make it, and help me to be kind and loving to all people. Use me in the mainstream of life, and remove worry, remorse, and morbid reflection that I may be of service to others. Amen.

When I retire at night...   /   /

Chronology of today's events:

Was I resentful?
    1. *Who/what*   3. *Affects*

    2. *Cause*   4. *My part*

Was I selfish?

Was I dishonest?

Was I afraid?

Do I owe an apology?

What have I wrongly kept secret?

Was I kind and loving toward all?

What could I have done better?

How did faith or fear rule my actions today?

Today I gave of my time ___, talent ___, treasure ___, and touch ___.

Who did I help today?

What am I grateful for today?

Who needs my prayers today?

God, forgive me where I have been resentful, selfish, dishonest, or afraid today. Help me not to keep anything to myself, but to discuss it openly with another person. Show me where I owe an apology and help me make it, and help me to be kind and loving to all people. Use me in the mainstream of life, and remove worry, remorse, and morbid reflection that I may be of service to others. Amen.

When I retire at night...   /   /

Chronology of today's events:

Was I resentful?
    1. *Who/what*   3. *Affects*

    2. *Cause*   4. *My part*

Was I selfish?

Was I dishonest?

Was I afraid?

Do I owe an apology?

What have I wrongly kept secret?

Was I kind and loving toward all?

What could I have done better?

How did faith or fear rule my actions today?

Today I gave of my time ___, talent ___, treasure ___, and touch ___.

Who did I help today?

What am I grateful for today?

Who needs my prayers today?

God, forgive me where I have been resentful, selfish, dishonest, or afraid today. Help me not to keep anything to myself, but to discuss it openly with another person. Show me where I owe an apology and help me make it, and help me to be kind and loving to all people. Use me in the mainstream of life, and remove worry, remorse, and morbid reflection that I may be of service to others. Amen.

When I retire at night...   /   /

Chronology of today's events:

Was I resentful?
    1. Who/what   *3. Affects*

    2. Cause   *4. My part*

Was I selfish?

Was I dishonest?

Was I afraid?

Do I owe an apology?

What have I wrongly kept secret?

Was I kind and loving toward all?

What could I have done better?

How did faith or fear rule my actions today?

Today I gave of my time ___, talent ___, treasure ___, and touch ___.

Who did I help today?

What am I grateful for today?

Who needs my prayers today?

God, forgive me where I have been resentful, selfish, dishonest, or afraid today. Help me not to keep anything to myself, but to discuss it openly with another person. Show me where I owe an apology and help me make it, and help me to be kind and loving to all people. Use me in the mainstream of life, and remove worry, remorse, and morbid reflection that I may be of service to others. Amen.

When I retire at night...   /   /

Chronology of today's events:

Was I resentful?
    1. *Who/what*   3. *Affects*

    2. *Cause*   4. *My part*

Was I selfish?

Was I dishonest?

Was I afraid?

Do I owe an apology?

What have I wrongly kept secret?

Was I kind and loving toward all?

What could I have done better?

How did faith or fear rule my actions today?

Today I gave of my time ___, talent ___, treasure ___, and touch ___.

Who did I help today?

What am I grateful for today?

Who needs my prayers today?

God, forgive me where I have been resentful, selfish, dishonest, or afraid today. Help me not to keep anything to myself, but to discuss it openly with another person. Show me where I owe an apology and help me make it, and help me to be kind and loving to all people. Use me in the mainstream of life, and remove worry, remorse, and morbid reflection that I may be of service to others. Amen.